MOUSE TALES AND OTHER ASSORTED STORIES

VICKI W. FOWLER, DVM

Inspiring Voices®
A Service of Guideposts

Inspiring Voices books may be ordered through booksellers or by contacting:

Inspiring Voices
1663 Liberty Drive
Bloomington, IN 47403
www.inspiringvoices.com
1 (866) 697-5313

Because of the dynamic nature of the Internet, any web addresses or links contained in this book may have changed since publication and may no longer be valid. The views expressed in this work are solely those of the author and do not necessarily reflect the views of the publisher, and the publisher hereby disclaims any responsibility for them.

Any people depicted in stock imagery provided by Thinkstock are models, and such images are being used for illustrative purposes only. Certain stock imagery © Thinkstock.

ISBN: 978-1-4624-0882-5 (sc)
ISBN: 978-1-4624-0883-2 (e)

Library of Congress Control Number: 2014900554

Printed in the United States of America.

Inspiring Voices rev. date: 02/10/2014

CONTENTS

INTRODUCTION

I spent years thinking about writing this book, and I finally wrote it after retiring. It was part of the grieving process. You see, I had spent years looking forward to being retired—and yes, retirement is wonderful—but I had to retire earlier than planned for health reasons, and I miss the wonderful people and pets that were Wynantskill Veterinary Clinic.

To those of you who read this book without living in my area and knowing any of the people or animals in the stories, let me assure you that the stories are real. These are the people and animals who have graced my life and who were there for me through the death of a child, a divorce, the raising of my children, deaths of pets, health problems, and retirement. They have shared in my joy and my sorrow, and I in theirs.

For the most part, I have changed the names of the clients and their pets, but I expect that many will recognize themselves on these pages. My apologies if your memory is not quite the same as mine. Also, there were many other stories that could have been included. Please know that all those memories are precious to me, but I had to stop writing somewhere.

This book is my tribute to all the people—both clients and staff—who made the clinic the unique community of love that supported me economically and emotionally for thirty-four years. These stories are why I would do it all over again without hesitation. My life has truly been blessed by belonging to such a loving community.

Again, thank you all, and may God continue to bless you.

MOUSE ORIGINS

This book is named after a cat named Mouse, who owned me and ran my veterinary business for sixteen years. He arrived at the clinic in the early years of my practice, when he was about nine months old. His owner brought him in for euthanasia, because he was "a dirty cat." I tried unsuccessfully to explain to the man that neutering the cat would almost certainly stop the spraying of urine that he was understandably unwilling to tolerate. The man wanted no part of my explanation, insisting that I put the cat to sleep.

I compromised by offering to take the cat at no charge to him, as opposed to charging him for killing and disposing of the cat, if he would sign ownership over to me. He gladly agreed, and I found myself in possession of—or, as it turned out, possessed by—a gray male cat with a white bib and white paws.

Mouse, as his previous owner had named him, needed to have an abscess treated and be neutered and vaccinated. After that, I would be ready to put him in a cage in the waiting room so that some client would find him irresistible and take him home. As sometimes happens, a respiratory infection epidemic swept the clinic that summer, and Mouse came down with a nasty infection. Our treatments were much more limited in those days; it was several weeks before Mouse was well. By that time, my employees had informed me that Mouse was here to stay as official clinic mascot. As I recall, they said something like "Mouse stays or we all quit."

He took his role very seriously, sleeping in the waiting room, supervising the feeding and walking of patients, greeting owners in the parking lot, and generally getting into everything. In the sixteen years that he lived at the clinic, I saw one client put him out of a chair and two clients share a chair with him; otherwise, the clients stood and the cat slept blissfully on the waiting room chairs. If you were sitting in the one that he currently felt was his personal chair, he would come over and stare at you. Frequently clients would stand up and give the cat the chair.

If staff were walking dogs in the side field, Mouse would accompany them, especially if the dog liked to chase cats and would drag the staff around the field while barking furiously. Mouse always trusted that staff would manage to hold on to their end of the leash, and he taunted the dogs by staying just out of reach. If people were putting food in dishes, he had to see if it was a kind of food he'd like to eat, and he wandered the kennel counters freely. He was not particularly interested in surgery but loved office calls and was known to come into exam rooms and wind around clients' legs to be petted.

Mouse always seemed in control. If he was running, it was for the joy of moving, not because he was frightened. If he was sleeping, it was beneath his dignity to acknowledge the chaos around him. If he allowed you to pet him, it was because it was his due, not because cats are supposed to like being petted. He ate staff lunches, batted pens off the receptionist's desk, and did a hundred other annoying things, and nobody ever took offense.

The cover of this book is a black-and-white photograph of Mouse sitting on a porch railing while looking smug. It was taken by a client. The photo was framed by another client, and the black ink footprints of a third client's cat (which she had adopted from the clinic) grace the white matting. It hung in one of my exam rooms until I retired.

I have owned (or been owned by) a long list of cats, but none was more memorable than Mouse.

TIPPY

My family's first cat was a gray tiger with a white bib and white feet. When I was six years old, during the summer between kindergarten and first grade, my sister, Louise, brought her home as a stray. Or something like that. I vaguely remember some argument about her origin and Mother finally deciding that she could stay.

The next big decision was what to name her. My sister wanted to name her White Tip Toes, but Mother vetoed that choice. She said that she couldn't picture herself standing at the front door calling, "Here, White Tip Toes, White Tip Toes, White Tip Toes!" So Louise settled for "Tippy."

Tippy was supposed to be Louise's cat, but Tippy hated Louise. She would lurk at the bottom of the stairs with her ears back and wait for my sister to come down. As Louise reached the bottom, Tippy would jump out and bite her ankles. I wanted Tippy to be my cat, but Tippy avoided me. Mother hadn't wanted a cat, but Tippy was hers, heart and soul. Tippy slept with Mother and followed her around the house.

Our next-door neighbor, Mrs. Stone, was terrified of Tippy, but Tippy would go and sit in her lap any time she was out in her lawn chair. Mrs. Stone would then scream hysterically until Mother arrived to carry Tippy home.

Mother explained at the beginning why all this was to be accepted without protest: Tippy was an enchanted princess. In great detail, Mother described how Tippy had been a beautiful princess enchanted by an evil sorceress. Since Tippy was a princess and we were only commoners, it was our lot in life to wait on her. We were to grant her every whim. If she asked to go out, we were to hold the door open until she finally went through. (Anyone who has had a cat knows that that can be a long time.) If she wanted in, we were to go back and open the door again. If she was hungry, we were to feed her. If she was sleeping, we could not disturb her. If I left anything, even my best clothes, lying around, Tippy had every right to sleep on them. We were her servants; she was royalty. Tippy, of course, expected no less. She lived in our house for eighteen years and never once hinted that Mother had been wrong in her assessment of Tippy's origins.

The only baffling thing was her choice of a prince. Tippy chased every cat out of our yard, except one. His name was Barkley Crumb Kemp, and he was the most disreputable-looking, beat-up, old tomcat that you could ever imagine. Tippy was quite fond of him, and they would sit outside our front door for hours. That's not to say that they sat together, because they didn't. Our front step had concrete sides, rather wide and flat, that formed large platforms—one lower and one upper—between which the stairs themselves were located. It was the sort of thing you see at museums and libraries in big cities, only on a much smaller scale. At any rate, Tippy would be the lion at the top on the right, and Barkley Crumb would be the lion on the left. We were mere mortals who walked between them without being noticed at all. One night, my brother came home very late and let Barkley Crumb into the house, thinking that he was Tippy. In the morning, Mother found them acting like a pair of lions on the living room couch.

Tippy was a great mouser and brought Mother a host of small rodent trophies. She would line them up in a row by the front door. Mother said she should have saved the skins to make a mouse fur coat with squirrel cuffs and collar and a feather hat. It's not a very politically correct thought currently, but it was humorous at the time because fur was very fashionable, but far too expensive for our household.

However, Aunt Dolly did have a mink stole, which still had the head with little, beady eyes. She brought it only once when she came to visit and left it on top of the piano in the dining room. That was normally considered the ultimate safe place in our household. We children would never have dared to touch anything left there. Tippy, of course, was under no such restrictions, being a princess and all. She took the stole off the top of the piano—no small feat since the piano was a very tall, old upright. Tippy proudly carried it into the living room, producing shrieks of horror exceeded only by those of Mrs. Stone when Tippy sat in her lap.

Mother, thoroughly embarrassed but slightly smug, rescued the valuable fur piece and hid it away in the coat closet—a safer but less honored location. Mother later hinted that it couldn't have been a real mink or Tippy wouldn't have been interested in it. I believed her at the time. Now, though, I am sure it was real but was close enough to a squirrel or a mouse in smell to attract the cat. Of course, there is always the concept that princesses are supposed to wear such luxuries.

The most interesting thing about Tippy's hunting abilities was her self-imposed limitation to outdoor rodents. As a child, I had an assortment of hamsters, one after another, starting with a white one and including several in basic brown. (The fancy colors didn't appear until I was in college, along with the longhair variety.)

If you are ever trapped in a mine or locked in a prison, take a hamster in your pocket; if there is a way out, he will find it. Mine escaped with some regularity. Tippy would find them, and Dad would rescue them. Specifically, Tippy would tell us which piece of molding to rip off the wall to get to the hamster. It was not necessarily on the same level of the house where the hamster had escaped. Usually, it was a living room wall instead of the wall of my upstairs bedroom, where the hamster was supposed to reside.

Never did Tippy harm a hamster. If we had mice in the house, an uncommon but occasional occurrence, Tippy would corner it in a furnace floor grate, which Mother would remove and then carry outside. Evidently, Tippy thought that if it was in the house, it probably belonged to me, because she refused to harm indoor mice but was ruthless with outdoor ones.

Just this summer, in a box in Louise's attic, Louise and I ran across a large, beautiful, black-and-white photo of Tippy. Tippy was as pretty as I remember, and her expression was definitely regal. I wouldn't be at all surprised to learn that Mother had been right about her enchanted princess origin.

LADDIE

My folks didn't own a dog when I was little, but I have vivid memories of a couple of neighborhood dogs, the most notable being Laddie. Laddie was a sable collie and the epitome of what you'd expect a collie to be like. I remember being told that he was a reject from a show kennel because his head was too broad and his nose was too short. It made no sense to me then and still doesn't. Collie breeders in my lifetime have bred for narrow heads and long noses. They have paid for that decision by a very high incidence of inherited eye disorders. I think they also bred the smarts out of the dogs, and I give Laddie as an example that wide heads are better.

Laddie was as close to human as a dog could come. As a matter of fact, he was the best outfielder our neighborhood had when it came to baseball. Harvey, his owner, was a couple of years older than me. He was generally the pitcher. I can't remember if we had enough kids to man two teams; he and Laddie were good enough to make a team of their own, anyway. Harvey would pitch, and if you managed to hit the ball past the basemen, Laddie would get the ball and run to Harvey. Laddie was fast! Harvey would almost always get you out. I don't think we played using strikes, so you had as many attempts as you needed to hit the ball. It really didn't matter. Laddie and Harvey wouldn't let you get on base unless you were very lucky at bunting.

Harvey had a tetherball in his yard. It was like a soccer ball on a long rope attached to the top of a tall pole. The idea was to hit the ball hard enough to make it wrap the rope around the pole. You would hit it in one direction and your opponent would hit it in the other. Laddie played that with Harvey too, until Harvey accidently put his hand through Laddie's mouth when they were playing and ended up with a bunch of stitches. After that, Harvey's dad banned Laddie from tetherball.

We lived in a city and walked to the nearby elementary school. It required walking past six or seven houses to the end of the street, crossing a bridge over the subway tracks, walking the sidewalk along the edge of a big field, and crossing a street to the school grounds. (When I was very small, there was a second street at the end of the subway bridge, but when I was about ten, the subway was converted to an expressway. That street was eliminated and a longer bridge was built.)

Laddie assigned himself the job of walking Harvey to and from school. That meant walking Harvey to school in the morning, returning home for several hours, walking back in time to be there when the lunch bell rang and kids came pouring out of the building to hurry home for lunch, walking Harvey home, walking Harvey back for the afternoon session, going back home, going back again in the late afternoon before dismissal, and walking Harvey home again. My mother said you could set a clock by Laddie; he always left his house ten minutes before the bell would ring.

When Harvey had completed elementary school, he needed to ride the city bus to the high school every day. (We didn't have middle schools then.) Laddie adjusted his schedule to include walking Harvey back and forth to the bus stop. That meant knowing when Harvey would return in the afternoon. (I don't think Harvey participated in after-school activities much, or maybe Laddie knew which days. I don't remember that piece.) But he never stopped walking the kids back and forth to the elementary school. All the neighborhood kids would pet and talk to Laddie, and it was an honor to have him walk beside you. Eventually, Harvey graduated from high school and moved away to college. Laddie took to walking my father to and from the bus stop. (Harvey's dad owned a car.)

Laddie had one dog in the neighborhood that he disliked. The dog was a big male Boxer who killed cats. Laddie liked cats. Maybe they had some other reason for their enmity, but whatever it was, it was constant. The two of them would meet at a specific corner at the specified time each day to fight. I don't believe that Laddie ever required veterinary attention because of fight wounds. Eventually, the Boxer moved away. It was interesting, however, that the fights always occurred during the time that the kids were in class. Laddie never fought with other dogs when the kids were around.

During the years that the Boxer was part of the neighborhood, we had the only cat. All the others were killed by the Boxer. Our front porch had no stairs to the outside, so Tippy could jump onto the porch through the railing and be out of reach of the Boxer. Laddie would start barking whenever the other dog would appear on the street, and Tippy would immediately stop whatever she was doing and run to the porch. She never ventured off the porch if Laddie wasn't around to keep watch. They were fond of each other and would rub heads whenever they saw each other.

I have known my share of collies over the years, but never one as smart as Laddie. The big, fluffy, gold-and-white dog will always hold a special place in my heart. I wish every child could have a pal like him.

THE CALF'S BIRTH

Veterinarians are privileged to be present for the entire circle of life. When I was in veterinary school, doing farm animal calls, I witnessed my first birth. The baby was a Holstein cow.

We had been called to the farm because the farmer was concerned about the birth; this was the cow's first calf, and she seemed to be taking too long. There were four of us: three students and the veterinarian who was our instructor. The farmer was an immigrant and took care of his farm and animals much better than the majority of the farmers we visited. His barn was painted white, inside and out. The stall was full of golden straw, the walkways were completely clean of manure, and the windows were clean and transparent. The cobwebs were noticeable by their absence. I have never seen such an immaculate farm before or since. His cows were crisply black and white, without manure stains on their glossy coats.

Our patient was standing in a deeply bedded, large box stall, almost knee deep in clean, fresh straw. The veterinarian with us did a vaginal exam, his arm gloved to the shoulder. I don't remember whether or not he found a problem, but not long after his examination, a pair of shiny black hooves appeared. One of the male students assisted as he gently pulled on the feet, and in a matter of minutes, the calf emerged into the sunlit stall. It blinked beautiful brown eyes at this new world. The mother began to gently wash its face and body with her huge tongue.

I was totally entranced and exclaimed, "It's so beautiful!"

Everybody turned and looked at me like I was an idiot. I didn't want to know if they thought I was stupid to believe the calf was beautiful or stupid because I hadn't expected the calf to be beautiful. It was a magical moment for me.

Over thirty years later, with many births and deaths "under my belt"—births of animals and my own children and deaths of patients and my own family members and friends—I still find births and deaths awesome. We do not create life, although sometimes we are involved in its creation. We can take a life but frequently are unable to prevent its loss no matter how hard we try. When the births are joyful and the deaths are peaceful, I know I have done my job well.

WHICH WOULD YOU RATHER DEAL WITH?

People have often asked me the same question that I asked Dr. Robert Kirk, who was the head of the Small Animal Hospital at Michigan State University when I was a student there. The question is this: "Why did you decide to do small animal medicine instead of mixed animal practice (which includes farm animals as well as house pets)?" Dr. Kirk answered to me, "Which would you rather deal with: an angry bull or an angry Chihuahua?" My answer is not very different.

When I entered veterinary school, I loved horses as well as house pets and dreamed of being a mixed practitioner. But two experiences as a student in the clinics changed my mind. One proved to me that I didn't understand cattle enough to safely work with them. The other impressed on me how strong horses are, and that is the story I tell as the answer to the "Why only house pets?" question.

In Thoroughbred horseracing, most of the money is in races for two- and three-year-olds, and exceptional stallions are retired thereafter for use in breeding instead of racing. In the trotting horse industry, there is big money in races for older horses, so it was not unusual for owners to have their promising young stallions X-rayed at the university veterinary hospital to see if their leg bones had matured enough to be able to race without harm. It was one of those young stallions that changed my mind about horse practice.

The horse had been brought to the university early in the spring and unloaded near the weighing and holding pens that constituted the "exam rooms" for the large animal hospital. The clinician in charge of the case decided to admit the horse, so I was told to take him down the large corridor that separated the surgery and radiology area from the barns. As you walked down that wide hallway, there were several large rooms on your left. In the rooms where farm animal surgeries were done, there were huge hydraulic tables and portable large-animal radiology machines. The darkened rooms with padded floors and walls were where horses would wake up following surgery. On your right was a series of barns, some designed for cattle and some with box stalls for horses. I was told to take this two-year-old stallion down to the "C barn," three doorways down on the right, and put him in box stall C 10.

The horse walked calmly with me down the hall past the first doorway. That door opened into "A Barn," which was a cow barn. But "B Barn," the second doorway, was a horse barn, and in stall B 5 was a mare that evidently was in heat. She stuck her head out of the stall and called to the stallion. The translation probably went something like this: "You're the most handsome thing I've seen in weeks." His reply probably translated as: "You're not so bad looking yourself."

With that, he picked up his head and walked into B Barn to stand in front of her stall and flirt. I found myself hanging onto his lead line, about a foot off the ground. He was not upset with me, merely totally oblivious to my existence. Even when I was back on the ground, I was unable to get him to move away from the mare's stall. It took a couple of my large male classmates to lead him out of B Barn and put him in stall C 10.

Thinking about what it would be like to deal with that stallion if it was angry with me convinced me that I would be a house-pet doctor. Today, we have good drugs for calming upset horses, and women horse vets are common. But I still don't regret deciding to stick with animals that aren't ten (or more) times my size.

ALICE

Back in 1972, when I was working for another veterinarian, a stray cat was brought in by the dog warden. The cat looked like a seal-point Siamese in body coloring and had the crossed eyes and kinked tail that were typical of Siamese at that time. But the cat, a female, had extra toes on each foot, a very non-Siamese trait. As a matter of fact, she had a different number of toes on each foot. She was brought to the clinic because she had been found wandering aimlessly, with a distinct head tilt that indicated a prior head injury or infection of the vestibular apparatus, which controls balance and is in the ear. She had frostbitten ears, because it was winter and the weather had been extremely cold. For some reason that I no longer recall, but probably because we were both young and starry-eyed at the time, I talked a friend of mine into taking the cat.

Pat's husband, Joe, who was less than elated, named the cat Alice, after a character in a television show. I've never been a TV watcher and was not familiar with the program, but I gathered that the TV Alice was not overly bright, and her husband spent a lot of time being exasperated with her. Pat's other cat, Cricket, was likewise not thrilled at the addition to their family. At times, Pat was not sure she had made a good decision in regards to keeping Alice.

For weeks, the cat wandered aimlessly around her house, mostly in wide circles, and would circle chairs. Her brain was obviously the worse for wear. Eventually, she did learn to walk with enough purpose to get where she wanted to go, although by a less-than-direct route on most occasions. However, there was also the problem of her ears. One day, Pat called to tell me that she had found a piece of dead ear tip that had fallen off in her living room, and I told her that the tip of the other ear would probably do the same. I was not entirely sure that either Alice or I would have much of a future, as far as Pat was concerned.

Cricket, come summer, decided to take Alice out for excursions in the backyard, which merged with an extensive area of woods. At first, Pat thought it was cute for Cricket to take her little sister on outings. Cricket, however, had been listening when Pat read fairy tales to her kids and was really playing the part of the woodcutter whose wife ordered him to leave poor Hansel and Gretel in the woods.

One day, she came home without Alice. Pat scoured the area in vain, and finally she put an ad in the local paper's lost and found column. A day or so later, a man called to say that he thought he had found her cat. Pat asked anxiously, "Does she have crossed eyes? Is her head tilted to one side? Are her ears different sizes? Does she have a different number of toes on each foot? Does she walk in circles?"

He responded, "Lady, are you sure you want this cat back?"

Pat did find Alice and brought her home. After that, Alice was not allowed out and eventually was given to Joe's sister, who had no other cat and adored Alice. I'm pleased to say that she lived happily ever after.

CRICKET

Cricket was not just an evil stepsister cat; she was also a loving, intelligent family member. She was the first pet that Pat and Joe had gotten as a married couple, which made her their first "child." Her fur was black and white, and she was always immaculate. 7

When they lived in an apartment, Cricket was kept inside, for fear of her getting run over. When the family bought a house in a quiet development, with woods behind the house, she was allowed out. Except, of course, in hunting season, when shots could be heard in the woods nearby.

As a first child, Cricket took a possessive interest in the human children that appeared in the house over time. She was quick to inform Pat and Joe when the babies cried, winding around their legs and talking insistently about the need to deal with whatever might possibly be causing the crying. If the babies woke during the middle of the night, Cricket would come onto the parents' bed and wake them. No baby monitor could have been more alert and efficient.

With the children, Cricket was always very gentle, and the three of them were all thoroughly attached to her. Other cats came into the home as time went by, but she remained the favorite.

Her only problem behavior, discounting when she decided to take Alice into the woods and leave her there, was related to the telephone. Cricket didn't like the noise of the phone ringing, or she knew that it was polite to answer it. Either way, if she was home alone and the phone rang, she would take the receiver off the cradle and meow into the phone. Since the closest relative was four hours away, Cricket answered a lot of long-distance calls. The relatives learned to call when they could most likely find an adult human at home.

Cricket was in her teens when she passed away from kidney disease. Pat and Joe have had other memorable cats during Cricket's life and since: Alice, Sam (whose original owner didn't want him after he lost an eye when hit by a car), and Mignonne (who claimed the baby's high chair and ate with her paw). And the children with which she played have grown and had children of their own. But Cricket is still fondly remembered by her family, and her vet.

PARROT SURGERY

One of the changes in veterinary medicine over my lifetime has been the development of avian medicine. When I was a senior in veterinary school, the university brought in a veterinarian from Chicago. He was the only veterinarian in the country in 1968 who was doing any significant amount of pet bird medicine. About a third of his practice was for birds, and he had established the appropriate drug doses and normal blood values for various species of birds. He spent one Saturday morning teaching us everything that veterinary medicine knew at the time about pet birds. So a year or two prior to opening my own practice, when a woman brought a parrot in to be treated at the practice where I worked, I was as close to knowing what to do as any other veterinarian this side of Chicago.

The parrot was a faded green color, its wings drooping instead of being held tightly against its body. It looked old, and with just cause. The owner said that her grandfather had been a sailor and had brought the bird back from one of his trips "around the Horn" seventy-five years before. She had brought it to the hospital because she had discovered a tumor on its chest.

The tumor, visible as an area without feathers on the parrot's breast, was the size of a large marble, with irritated areas caused by the bird picking at it, and connected to the breast by a stalk of skin. When I placed the bird back on the exam table, it walked slowly back to its owner, looked back at me, and cocked its head as if to say, "Okay, smarty, what are you going to do now?"

This was at the very beginning of inhalation anesthetics, and the hospital where I was working didn't have them yet. We used injectable, long-acting anesthetics for most procedures, although we did have some short-acting ones on hand. I had no idea what I would use to deal with the bird and wanted time to figure out a plan. We were afraid of bleeding because blood loss in a bird is often life threatening, so I took some orthopedic stockinet (think of it as a tube sock with the toe cut off) and created a shirt for the bird, to protect the tumor. I told the owner to bring her heirloom bird back in the morning for surgery.

When they returned the following day, the parrot was missing its "shirt." The woman said that it had pulled the shirt off during the night, and the tumor with it. I carefully inspected the area where the tumor had been and was delighted to see that the tumor was completely gone. There had been little or no bleeding, and only a tiny wound in the skin remained. The bird was just as active as the day before, so I assured her that the bird would be okay and sent them home with a sigh of relief.

JACK

My first Labrador was a black dog named Jack, who was given to me by friends in Tennessee. His parents were purebred Labs and lived across the street from each other. There were twelve pups in the litter. As adults, they ranged in size from forty-five pounds to ninety-five pounds, and only three weren't gun shy. Since Labs are supposed to be about sixty-five to seventy-five pounds and be gun dogs, I got my first lesson in the responsibility of the breeder to the buyer. Most of those people didn't get a dog that would have hunted or was the size they expected.

Over the years, I saw many people buy dogs of many different breeds that ended up not being what they had a right to expect. I also saw many people who purchased a dog that had too many of the breed characteristics. Specifically, they purchased a dog with serious genetic problems, such as early blindness, epilepsy, hip dysplasia, skin problems, heart disease, and nasty temperaments. Buyer, beware.

Jack, however, was my constant companion and protector. His loving heart started me on a lifetime of Lab ownership, which I have never regretted.

The first fall after we moved to the Albany, New York, area, I was sitting in the passenger seat of our car in a dark parking lot at the P&C grocery store in Wynantskill while my husband ran in for a few supplies. Two boys in their late teens walked up to the car, and one of them grabbed the door handle of the driver's door. I doubt that they had anything good in mind, but they didn't stay long enough to tell me. Jack came up off the black backseat of the car like a shot, only his white teeth visible as he snarled loudly. The boys turned and quickly walked away.

Because I had spent all my free time with Jack when he was little, he had learned to come, sit down, stay, and heel, both on and off leash. I would walk him across the Rensselaer Polytechnic Institute university campus in the late afternoons if I was picking my husband up in Troy. One day, there was also a woman walking her Yorkshire Terrier on the campus. Jack was off lead and went over to say hi. I wasn't worried, because Jack was not particularly aggressive toward small dogs. The terrier's owner was, however, and told me to get my dog away from hers. I said, "Jack, leave the cat alone." He immediately came back to me.

She was furious and said, "She's not a cat! She's a purebred Yorkshire Terrier!"

I replied, "He doesn't know what a Yorkshire Terrier is, but he knows what "Leave the cat alone" means, and we continued our walk.

Jack had an uncanny vocabulary. I wasn't a very good dog owner when I was in my twenties and did as most of the community did, which was let my dog run loose. We left the front door open when we were home, and the dog went in and out as he pleased.

One rainy day, my husband wanted to put on his overshoes and discovered only one of them in the boot tray by the front door. He picked it up, shook it in front of Jack, and said, "You stupid dog. You took my boots, and now I only have one." Jack left the house and returned with the other boot.

Several years later, when Jack was an old dog, we went on a vacation, and the teenage boy who babysat our dogs said that he would never do that again. The dog made him uncomfortable because, as he said, "He understood everything I was saying."

THIRTY-FIVE DOLLARS AND TWO BROKEN LEGS

Over the years, I have done only a few orthopedic cases. I generally told people that I didn't like things that "crunch," which was true, but only part of the reason. The main reason that I loved soft-tissue surgery and disliked orthopedics had to do with owners. You see, it generally takes about ten to fourteen days for a soft-tissue surgery to be healed, and at least six weeks (or longer) for orthopedic surgery. During that time, the care that the owner provides (or fails to provide) often determines the success of the surgeon's work.

The first two orthopedic cases I did when I moved to the Albany area didn't go well. Both were dogs that had been hit by cars and had broken legs. Oh, the surgery itself went fine, and the animals left the office with their broken bones properly aligned through the use of intramedullary pins. But the first one suffered delayed healing because the owners resumed taking him for long walks up and down hills and through fields as soon as he was released from the hospital. Instead of "restricted activity on a leash," he was running for miles each day on his broken leg. The second dog ran loose (unsupervised) all day and was hit by another car about two weeks after I set his leg. They took him to a different hospital to have the additional broken bones repaired.

The other extreme was the Johnsons. Mr. Johnson brought his dog, Spotty, to me with two obviously broken legs. He was very frank in talking to me. "I have thirty-five dollars I can give you to fix this dog, and no more. We love him very much, but I have two kids, and my money goes to take care of them. I won't let you put him to sleep. What can you do for me?"

To me, this was a reasonable question. Being a good owner didn't mean that you took food off your family's table to pay for your pet's care. I always tried to give people options, and to explain what the cost, advantages and disadvantages were for those options. Each person needed to do what was best for his family, not merely what was best for his pet.

Some fractures will usually heal if set with casts or splints, while others are less likely to heal. God was with Mr. Johnson, because Spotty's fractures could be splinted. Yes, the leg may be a little shorter, or slightly crooked, when healed, but it will be very functional. I explained the limitations of splinting to Spotty's owner: the legs might not be quite the same as before the injury; the splints must be kept clean and dry and not shift position for six to eight weeks; if they did change position or stay wet, they would cause damage to the leg instead of helping. Spotty absolutely had to be kept quiet and come back weekly to have the splints checked. If the splints were not clean, dry, and in position, I would have to resplint and would have to charge Mr. Johnson for doing that. For the sake of his honesty, his dog, and his kids, I would put the original splints on and do the weekly rechecks for his thirty-five dollars. It was a deal.

For six weeks, Spotty came in for rechecks, and his two splints were immaculate, dry, and exactly as I had positioned them. At the end of that time, I removed the splints and felt the legs. They both had strong bone calluses, indicating that they had knitted well, and were only very slightly crooked. Spotty walked well without the splints and went home, accompanied by two delighted boys. Mr. Johnson had kept his end of the bargain, and I had kept mine.

QUEENIE

Breeds vary somewhat over time in their physical characteristics and their temperaments. When I was a child, I knew a wonderful Doberman. When I was in college, they were too frequently nasty. Later, a temperament requirement was written into the Doberman breed standard, and most of them are nice now—at least in our area. The same sort of thing happened with Cocker Spaniels. At the time that I graduated college, they had wonderful, sweet temperaments. Now, too many of them are untrustworthy—at least at the veterinary office.

Queenie lived next door, with the Hammonds, when I first opened my office. She was a blonde Cocker Spaniel and as sweet as any dog I have ever known. There was no limit to the love in her heart for people, but her greatest love was for her boy. She would, much like the collie of my childhood, put Jimmy on the school bus in the morning and greet him when he got off the bus in the afternoon. However, that left most of her day free. She would hang out in her yard and watch the cars come and go in my parking lot.

I don't remember how soon after we came to the property that Queenie first ventured over. She probably came initially with Jimmy, who wanted to know if he could continue to ride his snowmobile on the eight acres. The property had been abandoned much of his life, and he considered it his playground. Jimmy was as nice a person as Queenie was a dog, and they were always welcome. He was one of the children who stocked my pond with small creatures, including fish, turtles, crayfish, and frogs.

But Queenie discovered that she was welcome on her own and would come most afternoons to visit. She would sit by the front door until someone noticed her and let her in, then sit quietly in the waiting room. People would pet her while they waited to be seen for their appointments. When it was time for the bus to return with Jimmy, she would quietly leave. Eventually, she became too old to make the trip, which was at least a thousand feet from door to door, with the house uphill from the clinic.

About a year later, Mouse took over her job as "greeter."

PRECIOUS AT CHRISTMAS

Veterinarians are often told not to get too involved in their clients' personal lives. It is supposed to break down the "professional" relationship between doctor and client. Since many of us spend the vast majority of our time at work, we see our clients far more frequently than our "friends." If you don't have friends among your clientele, especially in a small-town setting, you won't have any friends at all. Besides, our culture tends to erect far too many barriers among people. For those reasons, and because I'm just a talker and interested in what is going on in people's lives, I often was very aware of the personal lives of my clients.

One such client was Mrs. Wilson. She was past retirement age, although she had never worked outside the home, and her husband and her Chihuahua were her primary interests. They had never had any children, so the dog filled that role in her life. I always enjoyed talking with her when she brought the little dog in for pedicures or his annual exam and vaccinations. So I was aware that her husband and dog developed heart problems in the same year.

All this was in the early 1970s, and we didn't have a lot to offer dogs in the way of treatment for heart disease. It looked to me like the MDs weren't doing a whole lot better than we were, because the husband's heart disease progressed as rapidly as the dog's, and Mrs. Wilson lost both of them the same year. Mr. Wilson died in the summer, and the Chihuahua died a week before Christmas. Mrs. Wilson was totally devastated. For two days, I couldn't get my mind off the elderly woman whose house was now empty of everyone she loved.

There were three animal shelters in our general area at the time, one in each of three area counties. I called the one that I felt did the best job with its unfortunate wards and asked what they had in the way of lapdogs. They said that they had a Pekingese-Poodle cross, so the following day, I went to look. She was a sweet, little dog (not all dogs of that cross are, especially those that end up in shelters), her black coat curly and full of mats. She had ear mites and was not spayed but was healthy and only about a year old. I thought she would do. I purchased the dog and brought her back to my office.

One of my other clients, who had worked for me as a teenager, had a local dog-grooming business. I called her the day after I picked up the little black mix and asked if she could groom the dog before Christmas. Karen said that she would do her on Christmas Eve day, would not charge me for the grooming, and would pick her up and drop her off at my office.

The dog that Karen returned to me looked far better than the waif that I had picked up at the shelter. Her coat was shorter, but free of mats, and shiny and soft from her bath. Her nails were painted pink, and she sported a holiday ribbon in the shape of a small bow on her head. The dog herself seemed to be happier with her appearance, and was even friskier and friendlier.

When my office closed, I drove to Mrs. Wilson's house and knocked on the door with the little dog in my arms. Mrs. Wilson was surprised to see us but was happy to have company. She had been spending all of her time at various neighbors' homes since her Chihuahua died, coming home as late as possible to the empty house. This being Christmas Eve, she had come home earlier than the other days, because her neighbors were getting ready for Christmas.

She had been sitting alone in her house when I arrived, trying to get up the energy to fix dinner, and looking at the boxes of Christmas decorations that she had gotten out of the closet but couldn't bring herself to put up. She was curious about the dog and asked her name. I explained that the dog didn't have a name, because she had been found two weeks ago, wandering the streets in a nearby town. I said that she was badly in need of a home and someone to love her, and I was hoping that Mrs. Wilson would be willing to take her in. If so, I would be willing to spay her and treat her ear mites at my expense.

I left Mrs. Wilson's house without the dog, which had immediately been named Precious. She was clutched tightly, happily licking Mrs. Wilson's face, while Mrs. Wilson talked to her about how they needed to hang up all the boxes of decorations and fix a nice dinner. It was, after all, Christmas Eve.

JOE SALVATO

Courage comes in many forms, but my favorite definition was given to me by a Holocaust survivor. She said that her father once told her, "Courage is fear that has said its prayers." I am far more impressed by people who face their fears than by those who are unafraid. One of the bravest people I ever knew was the young man after whom my younger son is named.

Joe Salvato came into my practice as a child with a new collie puppy. Rover was one of my first patients, a beautiful sable collie with a true "Lassie" temperament. I cared for him through the puppy months and dealt with the usual problems. He lived a long life and was immortalized as the "two-headed dog" in the photo in one of my exam rooms. Joe had belonged to the photography club at his high school and had taken and printed a picture of Rover, which he gave to me as a Christmas present. The unusual part is that he printed it twice, with Rover facing first one way and then the other, on the same paper, so that Rover appears as a sort of a "push-me-pull-you" dog with a head at each end of his body. And while I have pleasant, vague memories of the dog, my memories of the boy are very strong.

Joe was a bright teenager who thought that he might be interested in a career in veterinary medicine. He applied for a summer job between his junior and senior years of high school, so that he could get a better idea of what was involved. The first thing he learned was that he was very, very, squeamish. However, he continued to assist me in caring for my patients, although he was often uncomfortable with what we were doing, even when that was something as routine as a vaccination.

Because emergencies tend to happen at inopportune times, most of my staff had gone home when the most gruesomely injured "hit-by-car" I have ever seen was brought to the clinic. That left Joe as the person who had to scrub in and help me in surgery, while the more experienced assistant ran the anesthesia machine and got me the things I needed. The corner of the bumper had caught the dog in the center of his chest, directly over his heart, shattering several ribs and ripping a gaping hole in his side. That should give you enough information to imagine Joe's role as surgical assistant.

Joe did everything required of him as I tried desperately (and unsuccessfully) to save the dog. It was not until after it was all over that he made a mad dash to the bathroom.

I have had lots of people work for me in the years before and since; only about half of them could have stayed in the room, much less actively helped with that surgery. Yet Joe was undoubtedly the most squeamish person I have ever employed. He stayed and helped, despite his own discomfort, as a sheer act of will. It was an incredible display of courage.

Unfortunately, I was witness to Joe's courage again about three years later. He was an undergraduate studying engineering at Rensselaer Polytechnic Institute when they diagnosed him as having bone cancer of the spine. Throughout the months before his death, he was calm and at peace. It was an amazing thing to visit him, because he, the one who was dying, would comfort me, the visitor. Despite his youth, his belief in God's goodness and love for him were unwavering. He would always reassure me that whether he lived or died was in God's hands, and he could trust God either way.

So Rover's picture hung in my office for much of my career. Looking at it, you would see an unusual dog. When I looked at it, I saw a nice dog, and remembered an extraordinary young man.

BRUNO AND TED

In the early years of my veterinary practice, I handled emergency cases both day and night, "twenty-four/seven," as they say now. There were no leash laws, and the majority of local roads were posted with speed limits of fifty-five miles per hour. We saw lots of animals hit by cars. I can't say that I miss those days, but there were some very memorable cases.

One was a big German Shepherd mix named Bruno. The call came in about three in the afternoon. My receptionist told me that a young man was on the phone, calling from the convenience store about a mile and a half down the road. He said that his dog had just been hit by a car in front of the store, and nobody would transport them to the veterinary hospital. Would it be possible for us to come and get him and the dog? We were not busy that day, or perhaps we had more staff then, or maybe I was always more gullible than average. At any rate, I told the receptionist to tell him that someone would be right there to get him and the dog.

When the driver returned with the dog and a teenage boy, it was obvious that the dog was badly injured. He didn't respond when I tried to check his neurological reflexes and was in circulatory shock. The driver said that the dog had been lying in the middle of the road in a pool of blood, with lots of people just standing around him. Instead of whisking the dog to the back and leaving the owner in the waiting room, which is my usual procedure, I allowed the boy to stay with his pet while I worked to stabilize the big, tan dog. Ted was never in the way; he never moved from Bruno's head, stroking him gently and talking softly to him. We put in an intravenous line; administered fluids, cortisone, and antibiotics; and treated wounds. The dog tried once to get up but was unable to move his legs.

When we were done, I told the boy that we would have to wait until his pet was out of shock before we would know whether or not Bruno was permanently paralyzed. Eventually, Ted's mother arrived, and I explained everything to her. She took Ted home to wait.

Over the next few days, Bruno regained the use of three of his legs. The nerves to his right front leg had been too badly damaged to return to function, so I amputated the leg about a month after his injury.

For many years after that, you could see him trotting around town, tail gaily wagging as he made his daily rounds. The only problem he had from being three-legged was that he would become footsore when he chased females in heat, and he occasionally had to be treated for blisters on his remaining front paw pads.

The best part of the story, however, concerned Ted. When his mother came to the hospital that stressful day, her first question was this: "How did you ever understand Ted when he called?" She told us that Ted normally stuttered so badly that he was very difficult to understand.

I never heard him stutter. Whenever he came into my office, he was so totally focused on Bruno's welfare that he spoke perfectly. With Bruno hospitalized for the first two weeks after the accident, Ted did lots of talking to me. From that time on, he stuttered less and less. Two years later, he graduated high school and began a career in the navy. He didn't stutter at all anymore.

THE FISH TANK KITTEN

Not long after I opened my own business, at the time when I was handling emergency calls every night, a young woman called, asking for care for a very small kitten that was injured. As it turned out, she had been grocery shopping that evening and saw a group of boys—not too many years younger than her—playing with a kitten in the store parking lot. What they were playing was a form of catch, with the kitten as the ball. She had astonished herself by confronting the boys and taking the kitten away from them.

Now she was assuming ownership of the kitten and the cost of medical care, despite the fact that her financial situation was limited because she had only recently stepped into the adult world with an apartment of her own.

The kitten's chances didn't look promising. He was about seven weeks old, thin, weighing barely over a pound, with scruffy fur. He sat on the table with his head down, unmoving. I examined him as thoroughly as I knew how and found no obvious injuries. His gums were relatively normal in color, no bones were broken, and there were no apparent neurological problems. He did seem sore all over, as you would expect from being used so roughly.

I admitted him to the hospital for nursing care, giving him antibiotics and fluids and putting him in an incubator made from a small fish tank with a heat pad underneath and a towel over the top. At barely a pound and a half of body weight, he was too small for me to be able to run intravenous fluids.

For about four days, I cared for the kitten, and the new owner would call about his condition. I couldn't give her much encouragement. The kitten refused

34

all food and seldom moved, sitting hunched over with his nose touching the towel on which he rested. He did urinate without blood, and his temperature was normal, but that was about all I could say that was positive.

In those years, it was very difficult to get blood work done on animals, except at the veterinary colleges. I could do a CBC (complete blood count), a BUN (a kidney function test) that registered "high" or "normal," and a fecal exam for intestinal parasites. With those three tests as the only laboratory work available to guide me in treating patients, I was forced to rely on a thorough physical exam, my intuition, what I could remember of similar cases I'd seen, good nursing care, and prayer.

The young woman and I discussed options and decided to try a blood transfusion, to see if that would provide anything that the kitten was unable to make for himself. When another two days had passed since the transfusion and there had been no improvement, I reluctantly told the owner that I saw no hope for the kitten. I requested permission to end his suffering by euthanizing him.

She sadly agreed. But it was the evening of my birthday and I couldn't bring myself to kill the kitten that day, so I put it off until the following morning.

Something needs to be said here about euthanasia. It is something that all veterinarians are required to do, because it is often the only way to stop an animal from suffering. Once an owner signs a consent form, or instructs the veterinarian to euthanize the pet, the veterinarian is legally obligated to do so that day. Owners commonly ask if any experimentation will be done on their animal before it is euthanized. (The answer, of course, is absolutely not.) It is a difficult time for both the owner and the veterinary personnel. In my practice, we would not euthanize an animal unless it was medically necessary or the animal was vicious; it takes too much out of a staff that is dedicated to saving life when you take a life for the convenience of the owner. So my postponing the euthanasia of the kitten was absolutely wrong, and I knew it, but I just couldn't make myself take the kitten's life that evening.

God does answer prayers. In the morning, the kitten was holding his head up off the towel and ate for the first time. I called the young woman and explained that I had been unable to bring myself to kill the kitten the night before and that today the kitten was finally eating. She was as thrilled as I was, gladly forgave my lapse of professionalism, and came to visit her kitten. A few days later, he went home.

Over the next couple of weeks, Johnny came back for rechecks and vaccinations, and then had no reason to return to my office.

I recognized the owner ten months later when she brought a cat in for neutering, but I would never have recognized Johnny. He was gorgeous. Today, people would say he looked like a Maine Coon cat. He was a big cat with long hair in shades of brown and black and a white bib under his chin.

He sat on the table with the air of a cat who knows that the world indeed revolves around him. His owner smiled and laughed with delight as I babbled on about how wonderful he looked and how nobody would have expected him to turn out to be so beautiful a cat.

Of all my successes, this is still one of the best.

THE SAINT BERNARD PUP

Back in the beginning days of my practice, there weren't any veterinary diagnostic labs (businesses that run laboratory tests on animal samples and know what the normal values are for various species of domestic animals) outside of the universities. If you were lucky, you were able to talk a local human hospital into running tests for you, but you would then have to call the university to have their pathologist reinterpret the results, because dogs and cats are not really "little people with fur coats." One such case was the Saint Bernard puppy that was won in a raffle.

Bear's owner had entered the raffle at the urging of his kids, who thought that owning a Saint Bernard would be wonderful. The father had reluctantly agreed to buy a ticket because he thought the raffle was for a good cause, and because he thought the odds of winning were slim. Twenty-four hours after bringing home their prize, the family found itself in my office, because the puppy didn't eat and wouldn't play.

On physical exam, Bear was much too small and much too thin to be healthy. He should have had a ravenous appetite but refused all food. Fecal examination was positive for hookworms and roundworms. His gums were pale. His temperature was normal. We drew blood and ran a CBC (complete blood count,) or *tried* to run a CBC. The procedure was to draw blood, mix a measured amount of blood with a measured amount of solution, look through a microscope at the resulting mixture on a special slide that had grid marks in a depression of specific size, count the cells, and multiply by a conversion factor.

That procedure was done for the red cell count and the white cell count. Then you looked at a stained slide under the microscope and counted one hundred white cells to determine the proportions of various types of white cells. We were successful at doing the red and white cell counts, which were abnormal, but when we tried to identify the cell types under the microscope, we were stumped. The cells didn't look anything like normal.

I called Memorial Hospital, a local human hospital, and pleaded with the laboratory staff to run a CBC for me. It was late Friday afternoon; they were not enthusiastic but reluctantly agreed to run the test—if I could get the sample there within the next half hour.

When the sample arrived at the lab, they immediately called and complained about the amount of blood I had sent. They had wanted a minimum of fifteen cubic centimeters; I had sent them three. I told them that the patient was a three-pound anemic puppy and that was all the blood I could safely send. There was grumbling on the end of the phone, and they said they'd call me back with whatever information they could generate.

About a half hour later, I received a phone call from the pathologist, who said that he had been furious that the lab had accepted a dog blood sample, much less an inadequate volume of sample, on Friday just before he was to leave. However, when they had looked at the sample, he had become excited, because the cells were almost all cells that should still be in the bone marrow and not in the circulating blood, and he was now very interested in what was happening clinically. I explained what I was seeing; he said that if the pup were human, it would have pernicious anemia.

With that information, I called the university and got them to track down one of the veterinary pathologists who had, no doubt, already gone home for the weekend. His diagnosis was autoimmune hemolytic anemia secondary to a heavy parasite load. That means that the puppy was destroying his own red cells because his immune system had become abnormal. The pup's survival was, at best, fifty-fifty. He advised that we worm the puppy; give it whole blood if its red count fell any further; give vitamins with iron, antibiotics, and cortisone; force-feed it; and pray. The owner was willing to try to save the pup, so we hospitalized Bear and started treatment.

For a week, the pup just hung in there. He didn't get worse, but he didn't get better either. Every evening, his family would come to visit and would bring him whatever they could think of that might be tempting. They would sit in the waiting room while I ran office calls and try to talk the pup into eating.

We had a doughnut shop in town at the time, and on Saturday morning, they came to visit with food for tempting Bear and doughnuts for themselves. Bear seemed interested in the doughnuts more than anything else, so they offered him a piece. When he ate the first bite, the family started cheering, and each of the children had to give Bear a piece of their doughnut. Bear found all of them tasty, especially the jelly-filled ones. My other clients initially couldn't understand what was so special about a puppy eating doughnuts, but when they were told that Bear hadn't eaten anything for days, they joined in the celebration.

Bear went on to become a 150-pound dog. He was sweet and clumsy and totally adored by the whole family. His owner sometimes laughed that it would have been cheaper to have bought a healthy puppy, and he never entered any more puppy raffles, but he frequently said he was glad he won this one.

Personally, I think the puppy was the real winner, because most families wouldn't have put that much money and effort into a one-dollar puppy.

CLEFT PALATE REPAIR

When I was first in practice, it was common to treat cats and dogs that had been hit by cars. Buster was one of those cats. Actually, he had not been hit by the car but had run into the tire, which sometimes happened when the timing of car and cat was just right. It meant that there was a lot of head trauma, but the rest of the cat was unharmed.

Buster had a concussion and a traumatic cleft palate. The roof of his mouth had split open down the center from his incisor (front) teeth into his soft palate from the force of the impact. We treated the concussion and waited to see if the cat would recover from the brain injury.

When he did, I was faced with trying to repair the wound in the roof of his mouth so that he could eat properly. Without the repair, liquids would come out his nose, and canned foods could get into his sinuses. This was not a surgery that was taught in school, but I enjoyed surgery and confidently attempted the repair.

Everything went fine, but within a week of the procedure, a small opening appeared where the hard palate and soft palate met. I allowed the rest of Buster's mouth to heal and tried again to close the opening. Again, it reappeared.

I tried calling the office of a plastic surgeon in Albany but couldn't get through his receptionist. Yes, he routinely repaired cleft palates in infants, but she was totally unwilling to tell him that I wanted to discuss how to close a cleft palate in a cat. This was very frustrating to me, because most doctors and dentists that I had approached for help with complicated cases were intrigued and very willing to help. As a child in Rochester, New York, I had admired a friend's father, an MD who was a specialist in internal medicine, and often talked with him and his wife about whatever was troubling me. So I called Dr. Clements and asked if he knew a plastic surgeon who might talk to me. He gave me the name and phone number of one in Ohio. When I called that doctor, he said that I should call the very doctor whose receptionist wouldn't put me through! I explained my lack of success on that front, and the Ohio plastic surgeon kindly volunteered to call the Albany plastic surgeon at his home.

A day or two later, the Albany plastic surgeon called me. He said that it would be easier to do the procedure and explain as he was working than to tell me what to do over the phone. So Buster had his cleft palate successfully repaired for free by a kind and generous human specialist who came, complete with surgical nurse, to my hospital.

I learned that the tension (pull) on the incision, which was what kept it from healing, should be relieved by making an incision in the roof of the cat's mouth over the hard palate, between the cleft and the teeth, and freeing the tissue in between from its attachment to the hard palate. The new opening would heal by itself. Essentially, the hole was moved from the soft palate to the hard palate, where the bone of the hard palate would protect the nasal structures and the hole could heal harmlessly.

Ironically, this procedure was published in a veterinary journal a few months later by another veterinarian, who had also needed to go to a local MD for help.

WHIMPY

Whimpy was a big chestnut horse with white markings, his back about six feet off the ground where the saddle rested. I've always been partial to chestnut horses and collected them as china figurines when I was a kid. Whimpy was my first live horse, acquired from a friend of a friend because he was no longer sound enough to be useful for shows.

I had a lot of trouble with Whimpy over the years. He was supposed to be "honorable" about fences and such, but I found that he loved to break out and take my other horse, an Appaloosa named Loco Pony, all over the neighborhood, especially to the corn patch of the neighbor across the street. Usually, these trips were in the middle of the night, and the police would wake me up with the information that the neighbor was angry because the horses were in his garden or that drivers were complaining of horses on the road. I had a fenced paddock with a loose barn (actually more like a three-sided shed) in which I kept my horses. When I was building the shed and it consisted only of posts and cross poles, Whimpy stepped through the wall to go and eat grass in an adjacent field. It was the most amazing thing to see the horse step over a bar and duck under another at the same time. I took to putting the horses in the shed and keeping them in with a bar across the doorway at (horse) chest height to prevent their midnight jaunts.

One of my most beautiful memories is of a crisp fall night with a full moon. I walked up the hill to the shed to check on the horses, which were in the shed with the bar across the door. Whimpy was standing at the bar, with his head out of the shed, ears pricked forward. He looked like a picture in the moonlight. I inadvertently stepped on a stick, which snapped with a sharp cracking sound. The horse came up off the ground, knees tucked against his chest, and cleared the bar from a standstill. He landed and raced off across the paddock, mane and tail flying.

Eventually, I built a real barn, with real stalls for the horses. The barn was some distance from the old paddock and a larger pasture area that surrounded the paddock. Whimpy and Loco would race around the perimeter of the larger pasture, running up the hill on one side, across the top, and down the other. Sometimes, especially if Loco was still at the barn and Whimpy was alone in the pasture, Whimpy would size up the fence as he came running down the hill. You could almost hear him asking himself, "Can I clear that fence? I could when I was younger. Do you think I should try it?"

I would go dashing out and put him in the barn and feed him dinner, or if it was early in the day, I would bring Loco to the pasture. They would play tag and wrestle like two big dogs, obviously enjoying each other's company.

I didn't know much about horses when I got these two, and they quickly became spoiled. Neither could be caught in pasture. However, both would allow my kids, especially my younger son, to walk up and pet them. If an adult tried to catch them, they would run off to the other side of the pasture. If you tried to trick them with a pail of grain, Whimpy would immediately come over to eat from the bucket, and you could hook the lead to his halter if you were fast enough. But if Loco got there before you had the lead line attached to Whimpy's halter, he would nip Whimpy on the rump and herd him away to the far end of the pasture. To get them out of the pasture, you needed to wait until dinnertime, when the horses would come to the pasture gate; you then opened the barn door and the gate to the pasture and stood back while the horses raced to their stalls for dinner.

There was a time when I had barn bunnies. My kids had figured out how you got baby bunnies, and I had about a dozen more rabbits than I could talk my clients into taking. I ended up turning them loose in the barn. You would look out the window and see rabbits of all colors out in the side field. They seemed to nest most often in Whimpy's stall. Despite his huge feet, he never stepped on any of them, and the mothers hopped in and out of his stall without challenge.

HOME FOR UNWED CAT MOTHERS

One of my clients once ran a home for unwed cat mothers. Honest. They lived in Grafton, New York, which is in the rural foothills between Albany, New York, and Vermont, and had no close neighbors. For at least a year, a brown tiger cat would come to their garage, when it was close to term, and deliver a litter of kittens in their box of old rags. She was not truly wild, because she wasn't thin, they could pet her, and she would allow them to handle the babies without moving them to a more hidden location. When the kittens would get to be about five weeks old, the mother cat would leave. The clients would dutifully place the kittens in good homes. A few months later, the mother cat would return and the cycle would repeat.

These were nice people, and they cared enough about the cat to feed her while she resided with them, and cared enough about the kittens to go to the effort to find them homes. They asked around town, hoping to find the owner, but were unsuccessful.

Eventually, they decided that the cat was theirs by default and should be spayed and vaccinated. They waited until the kittens were eating out of a dish, but not quite old enough to be abandoned by the mother, and brought her to me. I spayed and vaccinated her and sent her back home. She stayed with them about two weeks, until her incision was fully healed, and then she left again. She never came back.

The clients weren't sure whether to be pleased or disappointed that she had gone back to her "real" home and wondered whether the other family was relieved or disappointed that she never got pregnant again.

IRISH SETTERS

In the early years of my practice, Irish Setters were a popular breed. I had many of the big, red dogs as patients, but none more noteworthy than Mike.

Mike belonged to a man named Rich, who thought (and several dogs and a couple of decades later still believed) that Mike was the best dog ever born. The two were inseparable. Mike had a knack for getting into minor trouble and found himself in my office with some frequency.

To keep children busy and quiet in the waiting room, veterinarians try an assortment of items of interest. Some have fish, some have tables of toys, some have books, and others have games. At that time, I had a guinea pig in a long fifteen-gallon fish tank on a stand. He would squeak at people who approached, hoping that they would pick him up or feed him. He was more fascinating to Mike than to any of the children who came into the office. Mike would stand, for however long he and Rich had to wait to see me, in a perfect point, nose at the glass, right paw up, plumed tail stretched straight out behind him. And he drooled. Mike had visions of that creature as dinner. Guinea pig under glass, guinea pig steak, guinea pig stew, guinea pig with wine sauce—you name it. Rich would get a handful of paper towels to put on the floor under Mike's head, where a puddle of drool would form. The dog did it every time that he came to the office, for as long as that guinea pig was there.

Eventually, I decided that the water should be in the tank and replaced the guinea pig with fish. Mike was disappointed.

The other Irish Setter that I enjoyed seeing was Sean. Unlike Mike, who was a rough and tumble sort of dog, Sean was a beautifully groomed show dog. He always looked like he had just come from the beauty parlor, and while he was a happy dog, he didn't give the impression, like Mike did, of not having a care in the world. Guinea pigs were beneath his notice.

One day, I received a call from Sean's owner; the big dog was limping, and she was worried that there was something seriously wrong. He had been out in his run with a younger dog and come in holding up a front leg. The run was quite large and went down a hilly area that was wooded. Of course, I asked to see him right away.

He came in obviously favoring his right front leg. When I carefully examined him, starting at the foot and working my way up to the shoulder, he showed pain in the metacarpal area (just above the paw). I admitted him into the hospital for X-rays, found a cracked bone, and applied a splint. The owner was instructed to return weekly for me to check the splint, and the dog was sent home.

It usually takes four to six weeks for a bone to heal, so I saw a lot of Sean. Each week, he would come in, and I would check the splint to be sure it was clean, dry, still properly positioned, and unchewed. After three weeks, I removed it, checked the foot by feeling it carefully, and replaced the splint.

After six weeks, the bone had knitted and the splint was no longer necessary. Sean had healed beautifully and was able to resume his career as a show dog. However, for the rest of his life, the dog limped at my office, and only at my office. He would hop out of the car and prance across the parking lot. But in my office, he limped pitifully, beginning as he walked through the door of the building and ending when he crossed that threshold on the way home.

For years, we observed a ritual at each office visit. I would hold his paw and tell him what a good boy he had been all those weeks that he had worn his splint, Sean would wag his tail in agreement, and the owner would laugh at the two of us.

MOUSE GAMES

Mouse was never bored, or a boring cat. He always found ways to entertain himself. One summer, his source of amusement was pet carriers.

A client named Sue brought one of her cats to the clinic in a picnic basket. It was one of the wicker ones, with lids that hinged in the middle of the basket, so you could lift up either end. Her cat was safely ensconced inside, silently hoping that it wasn't really at the veterinary office.

Mouse entered the waiting room and saw the basket on the floor. He sauntered over and examined the outside. The cat inside didn't make a sound. This container certainly looked interesting, and whether it smelled like a picnic or a like a cat, Mouse considered the contents worth checking out.

He carefully lifted the lid with his nose and sniffed inside. Very interesting indeed.

As he slowly poured the front half of his body into the basket, Sue's cat simultaneously backed halfway out the other end, so that her tail and rump were hanging over the other end of the basket. All the while, she was voicing ear-splitting yowls of protest at a strange cat invading her hiding place. The noise didn't seem to bother Mouse at all, because he took his time satisfying himself as to the contents of the basket. For a minute or two they each occupied half of the picnic basket, although obviously not by mutual consent, until Mouse calmly backed out, not a whisker out of place, and strolled off. The rump of Sue's cat, the tail now bottle-brushy, disappeared back inside the basket. Grumbling noises continued to come out of the basket for some time.

Another client came that summer to pick up her cat, which had been spayed. She brought a cardboard pet carrier, with a soft, clean towel on the bottom, and placed the carrier on the floor in the waiting room while the receptionist handled the paperwork involved in sending her cat home.

Mouse came over, peered into the open carrier, and hopped in, settling down comfortably. The client responded by saying, "Oh no, Mouse. That's for Fluffy. You have to get out," and reached into the box to lift Mouse out.

Mouse promptly bit her, somewhat gently but leaving no doubt as to his belief that the carrier was now his. At that, the client responded by stating, "I'll fix you," and she picked up the cardboard carrier, turned it upside down, and shook it vigorously. Nothing fell out. When she turned it back upright and we all looked inside, Mouse was on his back, with his feet to the sides and his nails firmly planted in the cardboard. With a smug look on his face that could only mean, "I can stay in this box as long as I like," he condescended to allow me to remove him from the carrier. Fluffy made an uneventful trip home.

It wasn't just carriers that Mouse explored that summer. We received UPS shipments almost daily and sometimes were quicker than others at removing the contents and putting the boxes in the back to go out (initially in the garbage and later for recycling). Mouse occupied boxes in several stages of unpacking that summer, and on more than one occasion, an employee would reach into a reportedly empty box only to feel something furry. Mouse seemed always to enjoy their startled responses, sometimes darting like a shot from the box with his ears back and a wild look on his face, sometimes merely yawning and stretching to express his total unconcern.

After several of these episodes, we had all learned to look before we reached, and Mouse discontinued the game.

MORE MOUSE GAMES

Each summer, Mouse invented a new game. Having explored carriers and boxes, he moved on one summer to exploring cars. Clients would park their cars with the windows open and return after their office visit to discover a large gray-and-white cat sprawled comfortably on their front seat. He would reluctantly agree to leave the car when the driver pointed out that he or she already had a pet. Or sometimes, the client would be less observant, and the cat stretched out on the backseat would go unnoticed until they were partway home. Then the client would turn around and return the cat to the clinic, coming back in to the front desk to tell the receptionist about Mouse's latest escapade. One client actually got all the way home with the cat, which fortunately did not hop out to explore the new surroundings and was successfully returned to the clinic.

Sometimes, people left their dogs in the car when they arrived and came in to tell the receptionist they were there. Or they put the dog in the car before settling their bill, thinking that would be less disruptive of the office than trying to control an excited dog in a relatively crowded area. Mouse would take advantage of the situation to perch on the car's hood. The dog, of course, would take exception to that and jump onto the front seat to bark frantically and scratch at the dashboard. Totally unimpressed, Mouse would just sit there for some time, then slowly walk up the window, amble across the roof of the car, and sit back down on the trunk. By now, the dog would be totally hysterical and throw itself against the back window of the car in a futile attempt to displace the cat. People seemed to like this game even less than the cat-in-the-car game, partly because they were dog people and Mouse preferred to ride with cat owners. And partly because it tended to make a mess out of the car.

When waiting to see which cars would be left with dogs in them and which ones had transported cats and were left with inviting open windows, Mouse would perch on the roof of the porch by the front door. He looked like Snoopy playing the vulture, with his head hanging over the roof edge. Fortunately, it never occurred to him to drop onto clients or patients as they entered the building.

Another summer, Mouse decided to perk up the evening office hours with live animal shows. My waiting room was very small then, and usually crowded in the evening. It was easy for the cat to slip in unnoticed as someone entered or left the building. He would catch a baby rabbit in the field beside the clinic and slip in the door when the office was most crowded. Released uninjured in a room full of people, cats and dogs, the bunnies would run frantically around the room. Total bedlam would break out; clients would scream, and dogs would bark and jump at the ends of their leashes.

Mouse would sit calmly to one side and enjoy the show. A staff member would have to catch the poor, terrified rabbit and take it back out into the field, where it would gladly disappear. To my knowledge, Mouse never killed any of the prey he captured. Live ones were much more entertaining.

The only time I ever saw Mouse disconcerted was the summer that he decided to see how many dogs he could slap. He would walk into the waiting room, look over the dogs present, and slap one on the nose. He never put his claws out and never drew blood or left scratch marks. It was a "cats rule; dogs drool" sort of statement. Usually, he had judged right and the dog would jump onto or under a chair, yipping in surprise. Sometimes, the dog would try to retaliate, tugging on its leash and barking threats. Mouse would give him a look that said, "Get real," and saunter from the room.

Only once did Mouse totally misjudge a situation, and it was probably the client and not the dog that he misjudged. There was a large, male German Shepherd in the waiting room one evening, and Mouse decided that the dog was a perfect candidate for a slap on the nose. He sauntered over, cool as a cucumber, and hit the dog on the nose. The dog made a loud noise that probably couldn't be printed if I could have translated it from dog, and it bounded after the cat with the intent to do serious bodily harm. The owner was not prepared, or sympathized with the dog, and let go of the leash.

Mouse went flying through the exam room where I was working on another patient, with the dog too close behind. He slipped through the wooden folding baby gate that separated the exam room from the lab/pharmacy area just as the dog hit the gate. The gate, which was nailed into the doorjamb on one side and hooked to an eye on the other, held just long enough for Mouse to escape through another door into the kennel. A staff member slammed the door after him, and the German Shepherd, my baby gate looking like a fancy collar, hit the door with a bam!

The staff member captured the dog, removed what was left of the gate from around his neck, and returned him to his owner. We finished office calls. Mouse was invisible for the rest of the evening and was less cocky and more careful about tormenting dogs after that.

OSCAR THE CAT

When my younger boy, Joe, was a preschooler, he loved to watch the TV show *Sesame Street*. As you probably know, one of the characters was a puppet (or Muppet, if you prefer) called Oscar the Grouch. You only saw Oscar's head when he appeared, because Oscar lived in a garbage can. His view of the world was about what you'd expect from a character named Oscar the Grouch whose home, out of preference for that sort of abode, was a garbage can.

One day, when Joe was at the clinic, I saw a new client who had a cat named Oscar. I can't tell you what Oscar looked like anymore, or why she had brought him to see the veterinarian. But I vividly remember her interaction with my son, who, having asked the cat's name and being told that the cat was named Oscar, cheerfully stated, "Oscar lives in a garbage can."

The owner, an elderly woman who obviously didn't watch *Sesame Street*, was incensed. "Oscar is a very clean cat. I take very good care of him. He does not live in a garbage can!"

Joe was unshaken in his conviction, since he was talking about Oscar the Grouch, who *did* live in a garbage can. So he firmly repeated, "Oscar lives in a garbage can," in that "Don't tell me I don't know what I'm talking about" tone that all of us use on occasion.

The client repeated her disclaimer; Joe repeated his conviction.

I tried, totally unsuccessfully, to explain to her that Joe was talking about a character on a children's television show called *Sesame Street*. She did not want to hear it. For at least five, and probably ten, minutes while I examined her cat and provided whatever treatment was indicated, she and Joe argued. Neither the preschooler nor the elderly woman budged an inch from his/her stated position. Neither paid any attention to me or the cat.

When the office call was over, the woman took her cat home, still furious that she had been told Oscar lives in a garbage can. I never saw her or Oscar the cat again.

BUD BEAGLE

Over the years we had a number of clinic mascots, which I generally referred to as "the freeloaders." In the early years, there were as many dogs as cats, because they would come in as injured strays. In the later years, with the advent of leash laws, most of the injured strays were cats. Bud Beagle, an oversized beagle or a beagle mix, was one of those dogs.

Bud arrived at the clinic, with a face full of quills, brought in by the dog warden. He lived there from 1985 until his death in 2000. He considered it his job to train new kennel workers in the proper technique for walking dogs. Because I owned about eight acres at work, we walked the dogs on leashes in the side field twice (or sometimes more) each day. Bud loved these daily walks, and staff would generally spend extra time walking him around the fields behind the building, letting him "read the newspaper" with his nose. Everyone who worked for me during his lifetime has a story of how Bud managed to get loose to go chase rabbits. It was what he lived for. You could hear him barking for great distances as he ran through the neighbors' properties, chasing those bunnies. Eventually, he would return, tongue hanging out and smiling happily.

Once he was caught by the dog warden while he was roaming the neighborhood and taken to the pound. My staff was miserable at the thought of Bud dying there and considered it unlikely that a middle-aged beagle mix would find a good home. So they took up a collection among themselves, and one of them went out at lunchtime to bail him out and bring him home to the clinic.

Bud loved being outside, so we put up a dog trolley for him outside the back door, running from the door to the barn. In good weather, Bud and a large bowl of water would be put out for much of the day. He loved to lie there in the shade, watching the comings and goings of people and pets. In the winter, he would be out briefly and play king of the hill on the mounds of snow that the plow had removed from the employee parking area.

The trolley was why he was still able to train new employees as an old dog. You see, if you disconnected him from his leash before attaching him to the trolley, or better yet, took him outside by the collar instead of putting on a leash for the few steps to the trolley, he would twist and pretend he was going to bite you. Of course, he was too much of sweetie to ever actually bite, but new employees didn't know that. At the threat, they would instantly let go, and Bud was off and running.

Toward the end, this was more of a trot than an actual run, and at least one new employee was able to run fast enough to catch him before he disappeared into the swamp behind the back field. Mike Rice, who was the last of my employees that Bud trained, said that he really believed the old dog was laughing at him on the way back to the building.

PORCUPINES

Porcupines were common in our area, and dogs allowed to roam were frequently brought in to have quills removed from their faces and feet. Our record for the most quills was held by a Chesapeake Bay Retriever-Saint Bernard cross that required four and a half hours for two people to pull out all the quills. His face was totally covered by quills, except for the eyes, and there were quills covering his chest and both front legs. The worst part, from the owner's point of view, was that they had left the dead porcupine on their front lawn when they rushed the dog to the clinic. When they returned home, their other dog had a face full of quills from biting the dead porcupine, and it too had to be brought in for dequilling.

Dogs that tangle with porcupines do so repeatedly. One dog, named Queenie, was dequilled four times before the owner decided he no longer could afford the dog's trips to the vet. We placed her with a friend in a nearby city, where she was walked on a leash—and there were no porcupines. She did, however, enjoy eating out of the cat box, which she would drag into their hallway. After the husband installed a security chain on the hall side of the door, so that the cat could enter the bathroom but the shepherd mix could not, she became the darling of the household.

Another client, similarly tired of trips to the vet but not willing to give up his dog, bought a doghouse and chained the dog to it when he wasn't home. Unfortunately, the porcupine wasn't chained, and the poor dog was quilled while chained to the doghouse. The owner then bought tall fencing and built a pen for his dog. After that, we saw them only for routine checkups.

One of my neighbors had a dog named Winston, who was frequently brought in for quills. It really wasn't his fault. Another neighbor had a dog that would come by to get Winston, and they would go hunting. We think he used to dare Winston to bite the porcupine, because only Winston would be quilled. When the neighbor dog died, Winston's career as a porcupine hunter ended.

Quills are not without danger to the dog. I had one dog in the practice that was quilled while the family was on vacation in the mountains and was gone for several days. When she returned, they took her to the vet to be dequilled, but many quills were buried too deeply to be removed. Quills have microscopic barbs on the tip and only move in one direction. We removed quills that traveled through the chest and out the other side of the dog for months. Another dog in the practice actually ended up in an eight-hour surgery at Cornell University College of Veterinary Medicine to remove a fistulous tract extending from its head into its chest. There was a quill in the chest at the end of the tract.

The record in my clinic for the most quilling episodes belonged to a Great Dane mix named Brutus. Brutus must have come in a dozen times to be dequilled. Then the visits abruptly stopped. Several months later, he came in for some routine work, and I asked the owner how he had stopped Brutus from attacking porcupines. He replied, "I didn't stop him. He still gets quilled. But now I just say to him, "You are going to the vet. You are getting sleepy." And he lies down and shuts his eyes and I pull out the quills."

I almost believed him.

JENNY BROWN

One warm, sunny Sunday afternoon at the time when I took all my own emergency calls, I received a call from Mrs. Brown about Jenny. Jenny was a sweet, medium-sized mixed breed dog, and Mrs. Brown was concerned because Jenny had been "scraped by a car." She didn't want to bother me, and Jenny was acting fine, but she would feel better if I took a look at her. Of course, I told her to come right over.

When they arrived, I was totally unprepared for Jenny's appearance. Mrs. Brown was married to an MD, so I had assumed that a "scrape" to her would be a scrape to me. Not so. Jenny had a piece of skin the size of a piece of notebook paper that was detached on three sides. The muscles of the entire left side of her chest were visible. Granted, she showed no signs of shock or discomfort, behaving as her usual happy self.

I spent an hour or so repairing the wound. When she was awake from the anesthetic, I sent her home on antibiotics, and she healed fine, but I was again reminded that it is often very hard to tell what is going on by what the owner is describing.

In previous instances, I had owners tell me that their dog was bleeding to death only to arrive at the veterinary hospital with very minor injuries. Owners can and do underestimate the severity of a problem where there is no bleeding, such as those who think that cats that are unable to urinate are merely constipated. Also, they often are not aware of how much weight their pet has lost until the animal is extremely thin.

I have always admired those receptionists who are able to get enough information from a phone call to accurately assess how quickly you need to see the pet. A good receptionist saves animal lives by insisting that clients bring their pet in immediately in certain situations, even though the client may not understand the urgency. A poor, or poorly trained, receptionist will not recognize the need for urgency, and endanger the life of the pet because the owner doesn't realize what problem really exists. A good veterinarian treasures a sharp receptionist, and I have been blessed with outstanding ones in my career. Thank you Jocelyn, Jeannie, Kelly, Sue and Wenda for making a big difference in my life and in the lives of my patients and clients.

SAM

I have frequently teased Dr. Glennon, the first surgical specialist in our area, that he took all the fun out of practice for me. He knows I don't really mean it, but he did bring to an end the era where I did my most exciting surgeries. Prior to his arrival in the Capital District, you had to travel to Ithaca, some four and a half hours away in dry weather, to reach a board-certified surgeon. So if you had something unusual and weren't willing to travel that far, I could justify doing my best for you in surgery. Once Dr. Glennon came, it was hard to justify operating on cases where I knew he could do a better or safer job.

But before Dr. Glennon came on the scene, I loved soft-tissue surgery; orthopedic surgery I had never liked and generally referred. I handled an assortment of trauma cases and extensive tumor removals, developing skill in plastic and reconstructive surgery. At one point in the mid-1980s, I traveled to Auburn, Alabama, to do two weeks of independent study under Dr. Steve Swaim, who is arguably the father of veterinary plastic surgery. It was exciting to discover that I had learned by necessity much of what he taught in classes.

I also attended the annual Surgeons' Conference for several years. A good surgeon must know how to do anesthesia, how to treat and prevent shock, how to do good medical care of postoperative cases, and how to diagnose which cases require surgery in the first place. So the Surgeons' Conference is one of the best continuing education meetings in the country. I also took the American Society for Internal Fixation (ASIF) course in Ohio, which was (and probably still is) the most respected orthopedic surgery conference. The conceptual lectures on how bones break and how they heal were taught by Swiss MDs. After the lectures, the participants would attend separate labs for equine, small-animal, or human medicine. I wanted to be able to talk to and understand the orthopedic surgeons and to know which cases could be referred locally and which ones needed to go to a surgical specialist.

Sam came in during the time that I did "the fun stuff." He was a small, white kitten, three or four months old, that had been hit by a car and had suffered a "degloving" injury of his right front leg. Think of the skin of your arm as a glove. Now you know what a degloving injury is.

Sam had been degloved from just below his elbow to his paw. When you have a degloving injury and the skin is still present but pulled down to the paw, you can pull it back up and suture it in place. Unfortunately, Sam's skin wasn't there. So we treated the wound and waited for a "granulation bed" to form. That is when the tissue has the most blood supply in its attempt to scar in a wound and is the best time for doing a skin graft.

As luck, or lack of luck, would have it, the granulation bed was perfect at a time when I was away. I came back, and it had passed its prime, but I did a full-thickness graft anyway, using skin from Sam's tummy. It didn't take.

I tried again with a full-thickness graft, but again was unsuccessful. Each time, I'd get a little of the area to take, but not a lot. Part of the problem was that Sam was just too active. Even with a bandage on his leg, he would tear around the house like the kitten that he was. After trying seed grafts and mesh grafts with similar lack of success, I finally hospitalized Sam "for the duration." That made a huge difference, and we were finally able to cover his leg with skin and hair.

Sam's injured leg never grew as long as the others, but it was as furry as the rest and more than functional.

Somewhere in my boxes of memorabilia, I have a picture of Sam and his kids, with Sam wearing an Elizabethan collar and sporting a bandage on his leg. As I write, I am looking at a Christmas card from Sam and his family, drawn by someone in the family. It shows Sam with a leg bandage at the top of the Christmas tree, which is falling over, knocking off a bulb. Sport, the dog, is tearing up packages, and there are broken bulbs scattered all around.

It still makes me smile.

THE SNEERING TERRIER

Sometimes, you know just enough to get yourself in trouble. Sometimes, luck (or God) is with you and what shouldn't work does work. This was one of the good times.

Long before we had a veterinary surgical specialist or a veterinary oncologist (cancer specialist) in our area, a client brought in a terrier with a marble-sized lump on his face. I removed the lump surgically and sent it out for histopathology. (I have since learned to do needle aspirations, so that you know what you're dealing with before you start cutting.) This lump was reported as a neurosarcoma. I'd never even heard of one before, so I called a surgical oncologist in Michigan who had given me direction before and asked what to expect and what to do next. His advice was to reoperate and remove as wide and deep a piece of tissue as I dared. This tumor would be slow to metastasize, but would be very locally invasive, and if it grew along the nerve's pathway through the bone into the sinus cavity, it would kill the dog.

I passed all this information on to Spike's owner, who agreed to allow me to do what I could surgically. Because the oncologist had told me to be bold, I removed all the skin on that side of the dog's face, making my incision down the center of his nose, along the black edge of his nostril and lip. Then I went up, almost to his eye, and finally curved around his eye to the starting point on the bridge of his nose. It was a big hole. I took off everything down to the bone, and I even scraped the bone in the area where the tumor had been, to try to be sure that I got every trace of the cancer. Then I took a flap of skin from his neck and recreated his face by filling in the hole I had made and suturing the black lip edge to the lower margin of the flap. I tacked the new skin as best I could to his gums where I had detached the original tissue that made up his face.

Later, I understood that I had made no provision for preserving his salivary ducts. Also, the flap of skin should not have adhered to the bone of his face. Food should have gotten under my flap and created an awful infection. The blood supply to the lip margin should have been inadequate to keep that narrow strip of tissue alive. The lining of the mouth should not have grown from the lip edge to recover the flap with mucosa, and the part that made the new lip should have remained painfully raw. But nobody told the dog any of this. He healed without any infection.

The flap adhered to the bone where it should and became a lip where that was needed. Best yet, the tumor never reappeared. Spike's owners were happy with the surgical outcome, and so was I. The only imperfection was that the skin of the new lip contracted so that lip didn't fully cover his teeth.

For the rest of his long life, Spike looked like he was sneering, which is pretty much in character for a terrier anyway.

LILLY

Lilly was a harlequin-colored Great Dane. She was purchased at a time when breeders frequently killed harlequin puppies at birth, because the black–and–white pattern was considered undesirable for show. Mrs. Mitchell had paid a large sum of money for her nonetheless and was delighted with her puppy. Both of us noted that her coat was a little longer than one would expect for a Dane, but Mrs. Mitchell didn't care. Lilly had a wonderful, sunny disposition, and that was what mattered to her.

When Lilly was about a year old, Mrs. Mitchell received a letter from the American Kennel Club asking for pictures of Lilly. She took the requested pictures—front, back, both sides—of her big, black-and-white dog with inch-long hair and sent them to the AKC.

They wrote back, saying that Lilly's registration had been revoked because the pictures of Lilly and her littermates that they had received convinced them that the litter was not purebred. We weren't surprised. Since Mrs. Mitchell had never intended to breed or show Lilly, and Lilly was a delightful dog, Mrs. Mitchell never approached the breeder for her money back.

There was really only one major problem with Lilly: she was too smart and had taught herself to open doors. That meant that if the outside doors weren't locked, Lilly would come and go from the house as she pleased.

Fortunately, they lived in a quiet neighborhood, and the neighbors loved Lilly. She didn't wander, so she was reasonably safe. It did, however, mean that the door to the house might be wide open all day if you left and didn't lock up. Mrs. Mitchell was usually home during the day and learned to be very careful to lock all the doors if she went out. But the outside door wasn't the only one Lilly could open. Lilly was just as adept at opening the refrigerator. Mrs. Mitchell ruefully had a lock installed on the refrigerator, so that Lilly couldn't help herself to whatever looked most enticing.

Lilly's whole family firmly believed that the big, gentle, loving, smart, and ever-happy dog had been worth every penny of the purchase price, despite her questionable "family background." We never did learn what genes Lilly carried besides those of a Great Dane, but the combination produced one of the best dogs I have ever known.

MARY LOUISE'S HAMSTER

This isn't really my story, but it is a great story that one of my clients told me. Anyone who has had a hamster will appreciate it.

Mary Louise is the daughter of a wonderful Italian family. She is vivacious and told this story with great animation.

When Mary Louise's children were small, they insisted that they wanted a hamster. Despite her own opinion that any sort of rodent, no matter what color or size, was abhorrent, Mary Louise took them to the pet shop to buy them one. They picked out their hamster, along with a cage and the appropriate food and bedding, and started home. The children, the supplies, and the hamster, which the pet shop had put into one of those little cardboard boxes that look like the ones Dunkin' Donuts uses for Munchkins, were all in the backseat.

At five o'clock, Mary Louise, along with a host of other cars, was navigating our area's traffic circle, when the hamster succeeded in chewing its way out of the box. Immediately, the kids started screaming. "The hamster is loose! The hamster is loose! Catch it, Mommy!"

Mommy had no desire to personally catch the hamster, since she was terrified of rodents. She managed to keep control of the car as the hamster ran across her feet and headed for the dashboard.

Everybody was screaming as Mary Louise drove into the nearby gas station. She jumped out of the car and ran inside while shouting, "You have to catch it! You have to catch it!"

The attendant followed her back to her car, where the children were screaming, "Don't hurt our hamster! Don't hurt our hamster!"

The hamster silently stuck his nose out of the dashboard and disappeared again. The intrepid attendant spent several minutes blindly feeling behind the dashboard for the escapee before finally capturing it, fortunately without having to take the car apart. He put it back in the box and put the box securely in the cage.

The rest of the trip home was uneventful. The hamster lived out its natural life span and was buried in their yard, complete with funeral service. To Mary Louise's relief, her kids never asked for another one.

FEEDING BIRDS

One of my photo albums has pictures of a bird feeder from decades ago, when I lived in a rented, second-story apartment. We had a bird feeder in the living room windowsill. It was quite a large one and would hold several birds at a time. Our cats considered it their personal entertainment center and would sit for hours on the back of the couch, which was beneath the window, watching the birds. The birds evidently had figured out that the cats couldn't get through the window, because they didn't hesitate to use the feeder, even when the cats had their noses pressed against the glass. That is one of the photos—a cat on one side and a bird on the other, both wanting lunch.

We particularly enjoyed the feeder during the spring and fall migrations, when dozens of evening grosbeaks would swoop down and empty the feeder in a matter of minutes. They were large black-and-yellow birds, very pretty and very vocal.

When we moved into our own house, just before my first son was born, I put a window feeder in his second story bedroom window. He would watch the birds as I changed his diapers, which helped keep him still. One night, we were surprised to see a pair of beady, black eyes through the window after dark and saw the vague outline of a small mammal that stepped off into space when we turned on the light. One of my clients was a conservation officer, and I asked him what would be a small mammal, with black, beady eyes, that could access a second-story window feeder and would casually step off into nothingness when discovered. He told me that we must have flying squirrels who were accessing the roof by a tree then dropping down onto the feeder. After that, I left squirrel treats on the feeder as well as birdseed.

In later years, I had both hanging and freestanding feeders on the back porch, within inches of the window in the dining room. We would sit and watch the birds as we ate. My sons came to be able to identify the birds by both sound and sight. There were several types of seeds in the various hanging feeders, suet, and a table with squirrel treats as well. We learned what to put in pans on the porch to attract mourning doves.

When the boys were in Cub Scouts, I brought their dens over to the house to identify birds, and the other children were as excited as mine to see these beautiful creatures so closely. We had as many as fifteen different species a day as visitors to the feeders. Our usual birds were mourning doves, downy woodpeckers, blue jays, nuthatches (the boys' favorite because they walked upside down on the trees and hanging feeders), chickadees (we never quite got them to eat out of our hands), tufted titmice, starlings and grackles (I have a hard time telling them apart without a book in my hand), house sparrows, cardinals, rose-breasted and evening grosbeaks, goldfinches, and purple finches.

Occasionally we would spot something unusual in the yard, like a scarlet tanager, Baltimore oriole, or indigo bunting. Robins frequented the yard also but never were enticed to our feeders, even though we tried some nonseed items. After dark, the raccoons came, and we enjoyed watching them before rabies became an issue. Then I reluctantly closed the wildlife restaurant to avoid having rabid raccoons on my porch.

Each winter, I debate whether or not to resume feeding the birds, and each year, I reluctantly decide not to hang up the feeders. Where I now live, there are birdseed-eating bears fall and spring, although we rarely see raccoons. I do, however, make an effort each summer to grow in my garden flowers that will attract hummingbirds, and each summer, I say to myself, "Maybe this fall I'll hang the feeders out again."

MORE BIRDS

A few years ago, I read a science-fiction book in which the people of a planet had been forced to evacuate, and in doing so had been unable to take most of the other species with them. Sort of a sci-fi take on the story of Noah's ark. They lamented the loss of birds, and bird song.

I can relate to that sentiment, as I have always loved birds, and the yard seems so empty in the winter without the songs and splashes of color that the birds bring. Over the years, I have tried to learn to identify as many birds as possible by sound as well as by sight.

At the lake where I now live, although it was also true to a lesser extent in other homes, you can tell the changing seasons by the sound of the birds. I have lived in the East, South, and Midwest. I have lived in cities, the suburbs, and rural areas. Amazingly, there have always been seasonal variations in which birds I could hear. The lack of song is a sign of winter. When the chickadees, who love to visit feeders, change from a winter to a spring song, you know that spring is soon to arrive. Canada geese announce both spring and fall, as they fly in formation overhead. Summer is full of sounds, from woodpeckers to robins to noisy blue jays. At the lake, there is also the sound of what I think is a peregrine falcon; at my veterinary practice, you could hear red-tailed hawks.

For a couple of years, we had a lovely white-and-black pigeon that lived in my son Joe's room and flew in and out of his second-story window at will. The bird would fly over the lake for the obvious joy of flying, swooping and circling round and round, to eventually land on our roof. When you saw the falcon high overhead, or heard him call, the pigeon would immediately return to the safety of the house.

One summer, we noticed there were other, less colorful, pigeons flying over the other end of the lake. Later that summer, our pigeon flew off to join them. During the time he lived with us, however, people walking the road would often comment on how much they enjoyed watching him and thought it was nice that he could fly in and out of Joe's room. My response was that having a pigeon on our roof was as close to city living as I ever wanted to be.

There was a pond at work, dug soon after I opened the practice, to allow me to have ducks. Over the following thirty-plus years, I had Pekings, Rouens, Muscovy ducks, Indian runners and a few crosses that happened by accident.

My favorites were the Muscovy ducks, especially a female named Madelyn. Madelyn was a small, white bird, who was part of our duck flock when my older son was a preschooler. She was very tame and would allow you to walk right up and pet her. A man named Jim was my kennel person at that time, and she was his favorite too. When he walked out of the building with the food tray, Madelyn would fly onto the tray of duck food. (She was the only bird I owned at the time that could fly.) Jim would stand in the yard, ducks all around him, holding the tray with a breakfasting Madelyn on it, looking like a living St. Francis statue/feeder.

Wild mallards often visited the pond, but there were always too many dogs around the pond for them to be comfortable nesting there. We enjoyed their presence, especially in the spring when they were courting. They would bob their heads and quack at each other in a water ballet. The rest of the year, they were quiet when visiting, and you frequently didn't realize they were there until they took flight at your approach.

Blue herons and kingfishers caught the little fish, frogs, and turtles that inhabited the pond. The pond was stocked in the first year or so after I dug it by neighborhood children who released their catches there. The kingfishers sat on a low branch of a huge weeping willow that overlooked the pond and then swooped down to fish. The heron stood motionless beside the pond as he fished, sometimes standing so still for so long that several clients asked me about the bird statue by the pond. (There was a fence between the pond and the parking lot, to try to keep visiting dogs and kids out of the pond, so clients couldn't get close enough to scare the heron into flight.) Occasionally, we found small turtles with holes in their shells from the long, pointed beak of the heron. He used it like a spear, and it left punctures in the turtle shells. It was then necessary to treat the turtles like the ones brought in that had been hit by cars and had their shells damaged; we went to the auto parts store, bought Bondo, and glued them. When they could eat and swim, they were ready to be released into the pond.

One of my cats, now deceased, named Miss Phibbs (who had been a stray hit by a car), used to fish for frogs in the pond. One of our clients had brought bullfrog tadpoles from her own pond to stock ours, and they flourished as well as the smaller frogs. Phibbies would proudly carry frogs into the office; we would return them to the pond if they were viable. The years when we didn't have ducks were always good years for frogs. Evidently, ducks think frogs and tadpoles are delicious, because they were always scarce when the ducks were more than occasional visitors.

Other birds besides the fishing birds loved the pond also. There was an abundance of small willows along the edge of the pond, the kind that never get very large and whose fuzzy buds are rather small. The goldfinches and phoebes liked to nest in their branches. However, they didn't like to share, because each spring, you could watch a pair of goldfinches and a pair of phoebes do aerial combat over the pond, for the privilege of nesting there. Usually, the goldfinches won, and the phoebes moved to similar shrubs a little farther from the pond, where they could raise their babies in peace.

In the summer, barn swallows nested at the clinic in the garage that doubled as a horse barn. They swooped in and out over the horse's head to nest in the rafters. The barn has also housed grackles in the worst of the winters, including one that an employee named Edgar because he reminded her of the poem "The Raven," by Edgar Allan Poe.

Each fall, the grackles or starlings (I've never been quite sure which) flocked in swarms in the trees along the edges of the clinic property. They were incredibly noisy and then suddenly became silent just before becoming airborne. The flocks of birds swooped overhead, looking like they were practicing group maneuvers. I've always assumed that they would be flying south together and were trying to get organized. Sometimes, the flocks were so large that they covered much of the sky, and when they landed, they covered the half-acre side field. My employees said it reminded them of the movie *The Birds*. I always thought of the early years of this country, when huge flocks of many species of birds were common.

It is easy for homeowners to grow flowers and shrubs that attract birds and provide them with food and shelter. Even people who don't personally want bird feeders or gardens, or aren't able to have them, usually because they are apartment dwellers, can help preserve these beautiful creatures by being careful with insecticides and encouraging their communities to have public parks. Hopefully, we will preserve our wild feathered friends, so that my grandchildren's grandchildren will be able to tell stories about birds they have watched and enjoyed.

MATTY

Matty was another black Lab. He had an impressive pedigree. His mother was my Champion Groveton's Fun and Folly, and his father was the top Lab in the United States two years in a row and the highest-scoring Lab at Madison Square Garden.

Matty had a life-threatening case of canine parvovirus infection as a small puppy because the first vaccine against parvo wasn't very good and didn't protect any of the pups in his litter. As a result, he never filled out to look like what he had promised to become before the illness. He was, however, everything you could want in a dog, and earned his Companion Dog (CD) title for obedience. Since we both hated showing, unlike his mother, Folly, who loved the excitement of traveling and dog shows, I didn't go any further with him in obedience competition.

Matty was so well trained that I was able to put him on a down-stay in my pharmacy/lab area and he wouldn't move while I ran office calls. Other dogs could even come up and sniff him, and he remained where I had put him. On more than one occasion, when I had a critical trauma case and needed a unit of blood, I put Matt on a down-stay on the exam table, put in the blood collection line, left the collection bag on the floor, and went back to working on the patient. I would return later when the bag was full, disconnect the IV, and take Matt off the table.

As a small child, my older son, Ray, liked to eat his breakfast in the living room in front of the TV on Saturday mornings and watch cartoons. Sometimes, he would leave his dish on the floor and go back into the kitchen to get something else, or he would dash to the bathroom, or he would run to get some toy. Matty would take advantage of his absence to eat the unguarded breakfast. Ray would be furious when he got back.

To give Ray a better way of dealing with the dog, I took the two of them to Kathy Dennis, who was a local dog trainer and had worked with Matty and me. It took her two minutes to solve Ray's problem. She explained to him that the dog already knew "down" and "stay," so all he had to do was tell Matty to do that "in the tone that your mother uses with you when she really means it."

Ray gave Matty the commands in a tone that I sheepishly recognized as mine when I was just short of losing my temper, and the dog immediately obeyed him. From that point on, whenever he left his breakfast unattended, he first commanded Matty to "down-stay," and the dog never touched his breakfast again.

Matty would go anywhere with either me or my kids, and Ray often used him to balance the pedal boat. Our lake is small, and you can see someone in a boat nearly anywhere on the lake if you are standing on our dock. We purchased the pedal boat shortly after purchasing the summer camp, which is now my year-round home, and would let Ray go explore the lake. It was tremendous freedom for a small child. The rules were that you had to wear your life jacket, and initially, that you couldn't get off at anybody's dock.

After the first summer, we knew people, and Ray could cross the lake to play with friends. Pedal boats don't steer well when they are unbalanced, so Ray would put Matty in the other seat to balance the boat. Later, Joe would do the same with Matty's grandniece, Caper, who was also a black Lab. Labs were originally developed as a breed to accompany duck hunters and sit quietly in boats. They were also intended to be family dogs, gentle with children, but with enough energy to keep up with kids who are playing outside.

Children are born to explore the world around them. There is no better combination when you live on a lake than a Lab, a boy, and a stable boat.

CAPER

A "real" Labrador Retriever believes that its primary purpose for existence is to be with its person. Caper was a real Labrador.

Her mother was a granddaughter of my dog, Folly, and she came into our household when my son, Joe, was a preschooler. She belonged to him heart and soul, and they spent as much of their day together as the adults would allow. She even slept in his bed at night, under the covers, her head on the pillow next to his. (Motorboat, a cat, later slept with them, on the other side of Joe, her head on the pillow also.)

The kids stayed home with a babysitter one Saturday while I was at work running office calls. Joe and Caper had a wonderful day together, and I learned all about it on my return home by following the "trail" that they had left.

We had a low area next to our property, which formed a springtime-only pond. The neighbor on whose property it existed was unhappy about it and frequently complained that his property's drainage had been blocked off when they built our house. We always expressed our sympathy, but the house had been built twenty years before we bought it, and we were neither responsible for his drainage problem nor capable of correcting it. We did make a trench down the side of our driveway, which kept his "pond" from getting more than two or three feet deep, but that was the best we could do.

In the spring, spring peeper frogs would lay eggs in the pond. You could hear them courting in the evenings, which I thoroughly enjoyed. This day, Joe had discovered the tadpoles, and he and Caper had waded into the pond to catch them with a mayonnaise jar. I am sure that little boys have captured tadpoles that way since jars were first invented. Believing that he had the perfect place to keep them, he poured them, and a considerable amount of mud, into the fish tank with his guppies. Fortunately for the tadpoles, they were too big for the guppies to eat them, and they were happily swimming in the tank when I came home.

After their successful hunt, Joe decided to read to Caper. So they lay on his bed and looked at several of his books. That was apparent from the large amount of mud and black dog hair on the wall, blankets, and sheets and an accompanying large pile of books. Both of my sons loved being read to each evening. Our tradition was to lie on the bed and snuggle with the reader, which Caper must have enjoyed as much as Joe always did. I took the sheets and blankets to the laundry room and went to the bathroom to get the materials to clean the wall.

Evidently, Joe had decided when snuggling Caper that wet, muddy dogs smell. Because there was an inch of water on the bathroom floor, which made a squishing sound as you walked across the carpet. The walls of the bathroom and shower were covered in black dog hair as high as my shoulder. I didn't know how that was possible, but there it was. All of my clean towels were now wet and lying in a heap on the floor. My new bottle of shampoo was half-empty, as was my bottle of perfume.

When the babysitter had discovered that the boy and a now clean, wet dog were playing in the house, she sent them back outside to dry.

I arrived home to a very happy boy and dog, cheerfully watering the plants in my greenhouse. The floor of the greenhouse consisted of raised beds, with fencing for climbing plants at the back of each box, and a rod running the length of the greenhouse for hanging plants. The raised beds were flooded and full of dog and child footprints, with little shoots of peas and lettuce floating in the water.

Joe's happy smile and enthusiastic hug, and Caper's joyful greeting, melted my heart. I replanted the garden after dinner.

LUCKY LADY

I like stories with happy endings; this is one of those stories.

It is about a small, nondescript brown cat who was allowed to run the streets of Albany, New York. Maybe her people didn't know any better. Maybe they thought it was cruel to confine a cat to an apartment. Maybe they just didn't care. For whatever reason, Lucky Lady was left to run the streets.

This story actually starts with the dogs. There was an assortment of them, and they ran the streets also. Because there was a pack of them, and perhaps because they were uncared for and hungry, they decided that Lady looked a lot like lunch. They cornered her behind a garbage can in an alley.

This is where the story takes a happy turn, because someone kind and courageous was walking by and saw what was happening. He rescued Lady just in time and brought her to my clinic for medical care.

Since I've always been gullible, and since the rescuer couldn't keep a cat, Lady became one of the clinic freeloaders. We amputated her right front leg because it was too badly damaged; not only was there severe muscle injury, but the primary nerve had been cut. It took a long time to control the infection in the other wounds. We closed gaps in the skin and tears in the muscles. Unfortunately, there had been so much damage to the knee joint of her right hind leg that it was never right again. We spayed Lady, gave her all her vaccinations, and wormed her. On weekends, she was allowed the run of the place. Weekdays, she was either in the business office or in a kennel.

If your pet was hospitalized with us, we encouraged you to visit. One of my clients had a cat in the hospital and was in and out visiting. She saw Lady and asked Doug, one of my employees, about her. Doug, who went on to become a veterinarian, was especially fond of Lady and was more than willing to tell Donna all about how we came to have Lady living at the clinic.

Donna came back several times to visit Lady. She couldn't get over how this little cat, which had been through so much, was such a friendly, playful creature. Lady would tear around the clinic chasing wads of paper and hop onto chairs to sit on window ledges, despite having only two reliable legs. She was affectionate and loved to be held. Lady would always purr whenever handled. Doug encouraged Donna to visit Lady after Donna's own cat had gone home. It wasn't long before Lady also went home with Donna.

I began getting reports of Lady playing in the sunshine in Donna's garden, which was small but a safe environment for Lady. Donna worked out of her home, so Lady had human company most of the time. This was a far cry from the streets of Albany. Lady ran the household, slept on the bed with the people, and ate her favorite foods. She lived well into her teens and was loved by everyone who came to Donna's home.

Lady even left visible footprints as well as those invisible ones that special pets leave on your heart. The picture of Mouse that is on the cover of this book was professionally framed for me by a friend of Donna's. Mouse had died long before I decided to have the picture framed, and the framer knew Lady and her story. He thought that Mouse had been too much of a character to have a plain frame and that Lady was the perfect cat to leave footprints on the matting.

I have always been especially pleased with the resulting picture, as it commemorates two extraordinary cats.

NEIGHBORHOOD TALES

One of the advantages to practicing in the community where you lived, and living in a small community, was that you could keep better tabs on your patients. Owners were not always good at following the instructions that you gave them. This is a topic known as "owner compliance," and there have been all sorts of articles written on how to achieve good compliance from your clients. For the most part, I had an exceptionally good clientele; they took excellent care of their pets, did what I asked, and paid their bills, all cheerfully. It made practicing a pleasure. But occasionally, I ran into a situation where the directions weren't followed.

To appreciate the first story, you need to know what an Elizabethan collar, or "E-collar," looks like. These are variously described by owners as "lamp shades," "cones," "satellite dishes," and "hats." Dogs hate them. Owners hate them more, because the dogs bump into things, including the owner, while they are wearing them. They are large, plastic cones, which keep the dogs from reaching an area that they want to chew, and the veterinarian doesn't want them to chew. The nicest ones are transparent, so the dogs have some peripheral vision. In the early years of my own practice, I often made them out of plastic pails, with a hole cut in the bottom. The current, commercially available ones are very good. You are supposed to take a dog out on a leash when it is wearing an E-collar because it usually has no peripheral vision and can't see a car unless it's coming straight at the dog.

Before I had my own practice, and was working at a veterinary hospital about a half hour from where I lived, I operated on a dog and sent it home wearing an Elizabethan collar. Unknown to the owner, I lived in the same neighborhood. Several days after the surgery, I came home from work to see my patient running loose on the street, dutifully wearing his Elizabethan collar. It wasn't an especially fast or busy street, but it was very near the main street through town, and dogs are notorious for not staying in their own yards. I called the practice where I worked and got the receptionist to call the owners. She told them, "Go out right now and bring in your dog. You know that you are not supposed to let him run loose wearing his Elizabethan collar."

They did. I never mentioned to them that I had been the one to see their dog running loose; they never mentioned that he had indeed been unattended. I have always wondered if they guessed how the receptionist knew.

Another dog, many years later, that also ran loose had major skin problems, secondary to food allergies. The owners were feeding him a special diet, which didn't seem to help, and giving him several kinds of medications. The dog was always broken out and itching, and the owners were not very satisfied with the treatment.

The mystery was ended one day when my technician was at the local Laundromat and saw the dog come by. Hershey stopped at the little sandwich shop, two doors from the laundry, and the shop's owner came out and fed him a delicious plate of scraps. Several items on the "luncheon special" were on his list of forbidden foods. My technician went over and explained to the dog's friend that Hershey was allergic to several of the foods on the plate. She pointed out the chewed spots on the dog's skin, and the sore ears, and said that they were the result of his allergies.

Evidently, the owner of the sandwich shop stopped feeding him, or at least was more careful which goodies he gave Hershey, because the special diet and medications were much more successful after that. The owners were pleased that the treatment finally worked.

FRIENDLY

Friendly was an English Setter puppy that the Johnsons had purchased many years ago. He had a heart of gold, but the rest of him was made of something less valuable. The poor, little thing was shortchanged in the genes department and had poorly formed legs. Worse than that, because his conformation defects didn't slow him down much, was his allergy problem. By the time he was an adult, he was almost hairless, with angry pink skin, sore ears, and a constant itch.

This was before the years of RAST blood testing for allergies, and before the proliferation of "limited antigen diets" made of such things as kangaroo and potato. After some time of trying topicals, antihistamines, and cortisone, Mr. Johnson agreed to do two things: intradermal skin testing and a "food allergy rule out diet". That's more of an undertaking than it sounds.

Dr. Ed Baker, the "father of veterinary allergy," had agreed to come to my practice to teach me how to do intradermal skin testing. Friendly was one of the dogs that we tested that day. It required shaving his side, drawing a grid on him with a permanent marker felt-tip pen, and injecting a tiny amount of allergen into the skin itself.

Into the skin meant just that—the allergen must be injected into the thin layer of skin, not under the skin, or the test would be meaningless. Fifty different allergens were injected into fifty different spots, as well as a positive control in one spot and a negative control in another. If the positive spot didn't swell or the negative spot did, the rest of the spots were meaningless.

Obviously, the positive and negative controls were the first two injections. A row of spots would be injected, and then you would start looking for reactions. Usually by the time you were done injecting the first row, the positive control would have become a raised, red spot, while the negative control was merely a bump in the skin the size of a pinhead. Then you knew that you could continue with the test. Any injection site that became raised and/or red was a positive reaction. You would shine a pen light almost parallel to the skin, to see if the bumps had steep sides. If the sides weren't steep, the bump's reaction was considered to be a false positive. If there was any evidence of bruising, the reaction was false positive. Sometimes, you could feel the reaction easier than you could see it, if the dog had dark skin. It was also critical that all the injections be the same size. Remember that this was fifty-two injections, and the dog was awake because tranquilizers interfered with the skin reaction.

A list of antigens that had produced positive reactions would sent to the company from which the allergens had been purchased, and it would make up bottles of vaccine for that individual. Only ten allergens could be in a bottle. After the special vaccine arrived, the dog would come in for allergy shots. I refused to send the allergens home with owners for them to give, because there was a risk of sending the animal into shock; you knew he was allergic to the material you were injecting.

Friendly was lucky and only had one bottle of allergens. Some dogs had as many as three. I never used more than one bottle on any given day, so some dogs came in every other day to rotate through their bottles each week. The first doses were small amounts of allergen, and you gradually increased the dose. Eventually, a maintenance dose would be reached and the dog would come in anything from once a week to once a month for his allergy shot. Some dogs eventually didn't need the injections, some dogs continued them at some interval for the rest of their lives, and some dogs didn't improve at all. Most of the dogs that I tested and injected did well, which I attribute to Dr. Baker's teaching skill and protocol.

Friendly did respond well and was on allergy shots for the rest of his life. He began to look better, but it was probably the food allergy rule out that did him the most good. After all, if you are allergic to what you are eating every day, it's hard to make a lot of progress controlling your allergies.

To do a food allergy rule out, you started by feeding the dog only canned wax beans for seven to ten days. That meant no treats of any kind—nothing was to go in his mouth except wax beans and water. If his redness and itchiness decreased, you then added one protein from a list of sources. For example, you could add chicken that you had cooked without adding *anything* to it, or beef, or lamb, or rabbit, or deer meat, depending on what you could readily come by. Other protein choices were eggs and cottage cheese.

If your dog increased in redness or itchiness, you stopped the new protein and went back to just wax beans until everything calmed down again. Then you tried a new protein. Once you had established a protein that worked, you did a similar process to determine a carbohydrate. If you tried anything that made the dog itch, you had to drop back to something that had been successful, wait until the skin had calmed back down, and then try something else that was new. Your goal was to find a protein, a carbohydrate, a vegetable, and a fruit that your dog could eat without itching. The process took weeks of trial and error.

Mr. Johnson was successful in coming up with a balanced diet that didn't make Friendly itch. He and his wife spent the rest of Friendly's long life cooking for him every weekend and making up packages of food to be used during the week. It was truly a labor of love.

The reward for all the time, money, and effort that the Johnsons lavished on Friendly was seeing him grow hair, have healthy skin, and quit itching constantly. I have often wished that I had before and after pictures, because you wouldn't have believed they were the same dog.

There were other dogs in the practice that went through the same or a similar process. It was hard to convince an owner to do all this work, but the ones who did were generally pleased with the results. It was somewhat easier once RAST testing and special prepared diets were available, because the clients no longer had to experiment with home cooking for months before we could establish a safe diet.

One dog that benefited from the special diets was Sweetheart. She also received allergy shots for most of her life and lived on a special commercial diet. She was a Labrador Retriever, truly a sweetheart, and she loved to visit us even though it meant getting shots. Her family gave her carrots instead of dog biscuits as treats, since she wasn't allergic to carrots and there were no "safe" dog biscuits. We took to stocking our refrigerator at work with carrots for her to eat when she got her shots.

We even had a cat on a home-cooked diet. He had lip ulcers, sometimes called "rodent ulcers." We had tried injecting them with cortisone, and even surgically removed them, but they kept recurring. Left untreated, that kind of ulcer is capable of turning into cancer, so finding a solution was vital. We turned to home cooking in desperation and discovered that on chicken and green beans the cat was fine. He lived for years eating French-cut frozen green beans and chicken baby food.

Now there are excellent commercial diets for cats with food allergies, and veterinarians commonly use them for the treatment of inflammatory bowel disease and skin problems. Similarly, prescription diets of all sorts help many animals with a wide range of problems, from heart disease to kidney failure. But you have to give special credit to those people who, before the commercial diets became available, did the work to establish allergen-free diets for their pets and spent years and years home cooking those diets.

OF DUMPSTERS AND BUSHES

This is a story of dumpsters and bushes and boxes in the Hudson River, of parking lots and warehouses, of gravel pits, and of farms on back roads. These are all the places in my community that people have dumped unwanted kittens and cats.

The lucky ones ended up at my practice and were placed in homes. Our record was fifty-two cats (mostly kittens) placed in one year. The sad thing was that, even if you ruled out "the pound," there were humane ways to deal with unwanted animals; there was never a need to "dump" them. In our community, most people had excellent success in placing kittens and puppies if they spent a Saturday standing outside the grocery store, with a box of kittens or puppies and a sign that said, "Free to good home." Several rescue organizations in our area have regularly placed animals through "adoption days" at local pet shops. We were always willing to place kittens and puppies and helped our clients "re-home" animals that they couldn't keep. Many other veterinary hospitals have always done likewise.

During the early years of the practice, we often had stray dogs to place and signs posted in our waiting room about litters of puppies that needed homes. Bud, Katie, Jake, Silly, May, and Heidi all arrived as strays. During the later years, we took in very few dogs, but an ever-increasing number of cats. I'm not sure if that was due to the enactment of leash laws and the lowering of local speed limits so there were fewer injured strays or because I developed a reputation for being a "cat person." Either way, the number of homeless cats was always enormous.

My cat, Motorboat, and her sister were found in our business dumpster in 1991. I took her home, and she is sitting on my lap as I write this in 2008. One of my technicians took home her sister, and they currently live in Tennessee. Fortunately, we spotted them before the garbage truck came, so they weren't killed by the truck's trash compactor.

A young man brought in a litter of kittens he had found floating in a box in the Hudson River. My neighbor took one, which lived into its teens, and other clients took the siblings. Drowning had never struck me as a pleasant way to die, and we were all glad that the kittens had been spared that fate.

I personally bottle-raised a tiny feral kitten that a man had found under a board in a gravel pit. He discovered the kitten when he set the board up to use it for target practice. She is now a beautiful cat with a good home, but nobody knows what happened to her mother.

Two of the numerous warehouse kittens went to a local executive, who took them with her when she relocated to the west coast. Their mother had been allowed to live in a warehouse as a "mouser." When she was killed on the road, the kittens were brought to us to be bottle-raised and placed in homes. Other kittens in my practice had actually been dumped at local warehouses; some were adopted by the people who found them. A number of kittens were the offspring of cats, now wild, that had been dumped at the warehouses in previous years. Most kittens that remained uncaught were run over by the truck traffic in and out of the warehouses.

Kim, my licensed technician, always did a superb job bottle-raising orphan kittens and feral ones that people were able to capture very young. Her bottle babies were always sweet and cuddly, unlike the feral kittens that came to us after they were six weeks old. Those were really wild animals that became somewhat tame, but never really were attached to the people kind enough to take them. Or if they were attached to their owners, they were still terrified of strangers.

We also found homes for the box of kittens left in the Taco Bell parking lot. A Taco Bell employee had gone out to pick up the box and called us when she discovered the contents. We had her bring them in to be placed.

The young cats that were dropped on the clinic doorstep generally were hiding in the bushes when we arrived in the morning. Some of them were so frightened that it took us several days to catch them. Once inside, however, and no longer terrified, they generally were very friendly and could be placed.

A large number of my clients brought in animals that they had rescued. The "Hoover Brothers" were a pair of kittens that a client found along a road. He kept them, named them "Jay" and "Edgar," and referred to them as the Hoover Brothers because they were so hungry when he found them that they "vacuumed up" whatever he fed them. His elderly mother already had a house full of rescued cats, so he came by his compassion honestly.

Our rule was that if, for any reason, you couldn't keep an animal that you had adopted from us, you would return it instead of sending it to the pound. Very few animals returned, because Kim was protective of our waifs and screened prospective owners carefully. But my cat, Cuddles, came from a family that had taken three kittens from us. When Cuddles was dropped on their doorstep, they decided that three cats was their limit and brought her to the clinic. The husband said that they had taken three of my strays, so I should take one of theirs. Between the waiting room and the kennel, she put her paws around my neck and snuggled under my chin. I fell in love and took her home. She blessed me for nineteen years.

Fortunately, in my practice at least, the number of kindhearted adoptive families equaled the number of cruel abandoners, so these stories had happy endings. But the real answer to homeless animals has always been teaching people how to be responsible owners. The unwanted animals should never have been conceived.

MAY

One spring, the dog warden of a neighboring town called because she had just picked up a young mixed-breed dog that had been hit by a car. She wanted to know if I would provide first aid and house the dog until the owner could be located. I agreed, and she brought the dog to the clinic.

This was a nice dog, half-grown, the sort of dog you'd expect if you crossed a German Shepherd with a Beagle. She had bad scrapes on her legs, with areas where the bones were visible, but no apparent internal injuries. I treated the scrapes by cleaning the wounds and applying antibiotic bandages. The dog never offered to bite during what was undoubtedly a painful procedure. (Veterinary medicine has come a long way in just a few years; today, this dog would have benefited from our increased understanding of pain and pain control, and an array of pain drugs.)

In a day or two, we were told by the dog warden that the owner had been located and would come in to discuss treatment and pay the bill. We continued to care for the little dog while we waited to hear from the owner, impressed each time we changed the bandages by the loving, trusting nature of the dog. She was so glad to have any attention, even if it was painful. The staff fell in love with her and spent as much time as possible stopping by her cage to comfort her and reassure her that everything would be okay.

When the owners arrived, they verified that she was their dog, then horrified my staff and me by asking that she be euthanized. I immediately repeated that the dog's injuries were more cosmetic than dangerous and that she would recover with only a few scars. They were not interested in her injuries at all; the dog had been acquired to be a watchdog on their farm and was too friendly to bite. She was useless and should be destroyed!

There was never any doubt as to what needed to be done here; I asked if they would sign ownership of the dog over to me if I also assumed the cost of treatment. Predictably, I then became the owner of this sweet little mutt. We named her May, for the month in which she arrived at the clinic, and everyone at work proceeded to spoil her. Was someone on break? You could be sure May had a visitor. I gave May the veterinary care she should have had, spaying, vaccinating, and deworming her as her healing injuries permitted.

For about a year, May was the clinic pet. Then an opportunity came for her to have a home of her own. One of my nicest clients had to euthanize her elderly dog and wanted a new dog to love. I volunteered May. It was love at first sight for May and my client's son, and May finally had what she had wanted: a family of people to adore who also adored her. In fact, May was not satisfied to love just her family, although she certainly did that. And they loved and spoiled her in return. She even had her own chair in the living room.

May became one of several therapy dogs in my practice. She visited a local nursing home on a regular basis and was involved in 4-H. If you went to the 4-H exhibit at the county fair, there was May, the picture of a well-trained dog, lying quietly at her owner's feet while hundreds of people passed by. Except, of course, if someone from my office came along and said, "Hi, May." Then she would forget everything except how much she loved us, and she would shower us with kisses while running little circles of joy around our legs.

MAC

My family has often accused me of talking too much, and it annoyed you as a client of mine or you also enjoyed swapping news of what was going on in your life. So it wasn't unusual that I discussed with a client her mother's grief at the loss of my client's father and the family dog all the same year. Her mother was particularly worried that she would have to sell her home and move, because the neighborhood wasn't what it had once been and she was concerned about living there alone. What was unusual was that I thought I had a solution, whose name was Mac.

Mac, whose official name was much longer, was an eight-year-old black Lab who needed a new home. His owner, who adored him, had multiple sclerosis and had just entered a nursing home. Why the owner's wife didn't want the dog was beyond me. Mac had been successfully shown in both obedience and conformation classes, and not only had his conformation title (Champion) but also a CDX title. That meant that he would come, sit, down, stay, and heel on and off leash, using either voice commands or hand signals, and was a beautiful dog. He had been the constant companion of his owner as the man progressed from being athletic to using a cane, from the cane to a walker, from the walker to a wheelchair. Mac was extremely careful never to bump into people.

My client took Mac to visit her mother. The grieving dog, who had been returned to the kennel where he had been purchased eight long years before, and the grieving woman living alone in a house filled with memories were a perfect match. He was large and robust; she was small and frail. Both were lonely and delighted to have an adoring constant companion.

For five years, he was the guardian of her house, fiercely barking at anyone who came on the property, until the woman told him the intruder was a friend. She, in turn, spent hours talking to him and petting him as she went about her household routine and enjoyed quiet evenings at home. He never failed to respond immediately to her requests, never needed a leash (which might have caused her to fall if he'd pulled), and never tripped or bumped her. She was fond of saying that Mac was the best dog she'd ever known, and his expression as he looked up at her made it obvious that the love was mutual.

He died a few months before she did. The happy years that they shared allowed her to stay in her home almost to the end of her life. He provided the security she needed to live independently; she provided meaning for his life, since a good Labrador Retriever sees pleasing his person as the sole reason for existence. It was a case where life saved the best for last.

OMAR

Omar came to the clinic as a kitten hit by a car. A school bus driver had seen the small white kitten get hit, stopped the bus, and picked up the kitten off the road. She had handed it to the person driving the car behind the bus, who had been required by law to stop when the bus stopped with its flashers on, and ordered him to bring it to our hospital. He had dutifully done so. We treated the kitten for a fractured pelvis and gave him all the routine care that kittens should receive. Nobody ever came forward as an owner, so Omar became one of our resident cats.

All this was before the raccoon rabies problem, so our cats were allowed to go in and out of the clinic all day. They would go play in the fields surrounding the building and come back inside to mooch lunches and have dinner. We didn't let them stay out overnight for fear that they would get hurt.

I had lived in the clinic building the first three years of the practice being open, and our business office had been the living room and kitchen area. We had, in addition to desks, a beat-up couch where people took naps at lunchtime and where my technician's daughter took her naps when she was a preschooler. The clinic cats and dogs also used the couch for napping; the cats were especially pleased when there were people to nap with them.

The clinic cats were mostly good hunters, and it was not at all unusual to have them bring in their prizes. I was napping on the couch one day when Omar brought his prize into the business office. It was a sunny summer day, and the business office door was open to let in the wonderful summer warmth. I awoke to a cat standing on my chest, which in itself was not too unusual.

However, I'd never opened my eyes to see a half-grown dead rat hanging from a cat's mouth, barely an inch from my face. With self-control I'd developed as a child (by having boys try to scare me with frogs and snakes), I put Omar on the floor gently and without screaming. He couldn't understand my lack of enthusiasm for his present to me but agreed to trade it for some canned cat food.

Because our cats wandered the building during office hours, and because owners were encouraged to visit hospitalized pets, Pat had lots of opportunity to get to know Omar. Pat owned several cats and never hesitated to seek medical care for them when it was needed. Her older cats would come in and out for monitoring of chronic illnesses, and her young cats would come in to be neutered. She had more cats than most people could properly care for, but hers received excellent care. When she asked if she could add Omar to her family, we were happy to see him go to a place where he would be loved. This was another "happily ever after" tale.

BOBBY JOE

Raccoon rabies first came to our area in 1991 and changed everything. Now all strays were suspect, all wounds of unknown origin were possible rabies exposures, and all unvaccinated animals were a major health risk.

It was during the early days of the rabies problem when the health department was requiring euthanasia or quarantine (for six months) of all unvaccinated animals with wounds of unknown origin, when Bobby Joe came to my office. His owner was a girl from an area group home that dealt with troubled teenagers. I could sympathize with the difficulty of their job, having had two teenagers of my own, and I wanted to be as helpful as possible. However, in this situation, they had not come soon enough.

Sometimes, institutions that are supposed to help people do more harm than good. This tends to be the nature of institutions, which must function by rules in order to work at all and don't have the flexibility to do what might be best for a particular individual. In Christianity, we are taught that "we wrestle not against flesh and blood, but against principalities, against powers,... against spiritual wickedness in high places." *King James*—Ephesians 6:12

The house staff, who were supposed to teach the teenager how to be a responsible member of society, had looked the other way when she began to feed Bobby Joe and let him into the house. Because they were merely breaking the rule against pets, rather than advocating for her to officially own Bobby, the cat had never been taken to a veterinarian for shots. I explained to the caseworker, who had brought Bobby and his teenage owner to my office, that it was likely that his abscess (deeply infected wound) was the result of a fight between two toms over territory or some female cat. (I called this "brawling at the local bar over some floozy.") Neutering Bobby would probably have prevented his fighting. But since Bobby Joe had never been vaccinated against rabies, he technically could come down with rabies any time in the next six months. If Bobby came down with rabies, most or all of the people in the house at that time would need to get a series of rabies vaccinations. He fell in the "quarantine or euthanize" category.

The caseworker replied, of course, that the institution had no choice but to opt for euthanasia. Bobby Joe wasn't supposed to be at the group home in the first place, and the institution could afford neither the risk of keeping Bobby home nor the cost of quarantine in a health department approved setup.

Meanwhile, the girl clutched Bobby Joe tightly.

I was angry that the house staff had allowed her to have and love this cat but hadn't helped her be a responsible owner and get it basic preventive care. If they had gotten Bobby Joe a rabies shot three months before, when they first started letting him in, all he would have needed from me that day was a booster shot and some antibiotic pills. Now he was being sentenced to die, and the girl was being reinforced in her belief that nobody cared what happened to her.

I asked how long Bobby's owner would be living in the group home and was told that she would be there about five more months. When I asked her if she would still want Bobby after she turned eighteen and was free to live wherever she chose, she vehemently answered, "Yes!" I then told her that I would keep Bobby for her, test him for feline leukemia and feline immunosuppressant virus (FIV) infections, check him for worms and deworm him as necessary, vaccinate and neuter him, and treat him for the abscess. These were all the things that he needed if she was to be a responsible owner.

The caseworker repeated that there was no way that I could be paid for any of the work that I was proposing to do for Bobby Joe. I told her that this was between Bobby's owner and me and that I did not think it was right for her to lose the cat. There would be no charge for what I did, and the girl was welcome to visit Bobby any time that she could get someone from the group home to bring her to the clinic.

We took Bobby Joe to the back to our isolation unit and settled him into a cage there, with a litter pan and a towel for sleeping, and food and water. The teenager kissed him good-bye, thanked me, and left smiling, instead of in tears.

Bobby Joe tested positive for FIV and I explained to his owner at her first visit that he would live longer if she kept him as an inside cat. He would always be more susceptible to infections, and any infection was likely to become life threatening, but that with good care he would probably live happily for years as an indoor cat. She was comfortable with that.

We did all his routine care, and his abscess healed nicely. Over the next several months, she called frequently and came by to visit a few times, sometimes bringing another resident with her. Evidently, it was hard for the house staff to arrange for her to visit Bobby, because it didn't happen often.

When Bobby Joe's owner was due to leave the group home, she called me to say that she would be moving into her boyfriend's mother's house and that there was a large dog that didn't like cats. Would I be willing to keep Bobby a little longer, until she was able to support herself in a place where Bobby would be safe? Of course, I would. She continued to call and visit for a few months, and then she told me that she had an opportunity to take a job in one of the western states. Would I be willing to keep Bobby until she could send for him? Again I answered yes.

You needn't worry that this story has a bad ending. Six months after moving west, Bobby Joe's owner sent her boyfriend to the clinic with an airline kennel and Bobby's airplane ticket, and Bobby flew out to join her. The last I heard, they were both doing very well. The "street kid" became a responsible, self-supporting adult, and the "street cat" became a pampered indoor pet. Which, after all, is what it's all about.

WICKET

Wicket was Mark's cat. He was gray, the color people call Russian blue. Mark got him as a kitten, when Mark was single and owned a dog named Ralph. Ralph was a German Shorthaired Pointer. He found Mark when he was an adult, and Mark became his person. The three of them had been a family. Wicket and Ralph played together as only a big dog and a small cat can play. They slept together in a bed that Mark had built for them. I euthanized Ralph because of prostatic adenocarcinoma, with metastasis to the spine. That was several years before Mark and I started dating, and many years before we married.

The first time I remember seeing Wicket was for a small lump on his skin. I recommended removal and histopath, and we did the surgery with a local. Mark always tells this story because I required them to return for a postoperative visit five days later, even though Mark was a Red Cross first aid instructor trainer and felt he was capable of deciding if there was a problem. The recheck took all of five seconds and was done at the waiting room counter. I had long ago given up trusting owners to know if an incision was okay, but that's another story. The tumor, by the way, was benign.

Of all the cats I have known, Wicket was the most athletic. He was incredibly fast to strike when you played with him, to the point that you had to wear leather gloves if you were making the bed and Wicket was playing "There's a mouse under the covers" with you. He would jump onto the bed with such grace that your impression was that he had dropped onto the bed, not jumped up to it.

Mark had installed a cat door in his front door, so that Wicket could come and go as he pleased. The downside to that was that Wicket was a good hunter and would occasionally bring home birds. He preferred to bring them home at night, when Mark was sleeping, and release them uninjured but terrified in the bedroom. Mark would then have to try to shoo the bird out his front door. Wicket thought it was a great game.

I was not one of Wicket's favorite people when Mark and I started dating in July 1991; I was *the vet*. Whenever my car pulled into their driveway, Wicket would come shooting out of his cat door, moving so fast that he never touched the three outside stairs and disappeared until after I had left. Eventually, he would remain in my presence, but I was clearly only tolerated.

In the fall of 1994, Mark and Wicket moved to the lake. It had been hard on him to stay at Mark's place when Mark was spending less and less time there. He couldn't even go out and play because I had made Mark board up the cat door when the Mid-Atlantic States rabies epidemic arrived in our area. Mark had made him a window box that he could sit in, but it was rather small and not the same as going out.

Wicket was happy at the lake. Mark had enclosed the upper deck off our bedroom with chicken wire, so Wicket could go out a window, via my dresser and his transplanted cat door. He had the deck and our bedroom, and every night he slept with us. We couldn't allow him the run of the house because he didn't understand why my cats were allowed to be on "his property" and would attack them. Wicket was delighted with the porch and for several weeks would happily greet Mark's return by calling to him from the railing. At night, he went in and out as he pleased, snuggling in the curve of Mark's body, sleeping on the pillow next to his head, or slipping in between us. Usually, that meant that his feet were cold, and he'd warm them against me.

But in January, he didn't look right to me and was diagnosed with liver cancer by a specialist through the use of ultrasound. Because it looked encapsulated (very rare with liver cancer), another specialist operated on Wicket.

During the spring, carpenters worked on the upstairs bedrooms and gave Wicket access to the whole house by mistake. Unlike previous times that we had tried to introduce Wicket to my four cats, this time there was no fighting, so Wicket began to have free run of the house during the day. We locked the other cats out of the bedroom at night because Wicket didn't want to share Mark, at least not right away. In September, he did begin to let Cuddles sleep with us on occasion. It was so wonderful to have him be a real part of the family.

However, in late September, the cancer recurred with a vengeance. In early October, another attempt at surgery was made by the specialist. Mark and I went to see Wicket at the end of the surgery. Wicket responded to Mark's voice and touch. That night, Wicket passed away quietly in his sleep.

We had him cremated and sprinkled his ashes in the garden. His cat door, now permanently installed in the wall of our bedroom, and the porch, now more attractively enclosed, became his gift to the other cats.

BOAT

My Motorboat is often referred to as the only motorboat on Big Bowman Pond, which is the small lake where I live. The lake has always been motorless, first by gentleman's agreement and now by a town ordinance that we residents had requested a few years ago. My Motorboat is a cat. She was found at about six weeks of age in our dumpster at work, along with her sister. My son, Joe, talked me into bringing her home, and he named her Motorboat because she never stopped purring. She is the softest coated of my cats, has beautiful markings, something between calico and tortoise shell with spots like a Bengal, gets along with other cats and dogs, and loves people. She spent years sleeping with Joe, under the covers, her head on the pillow, stretched against his body and in the crook of his arm like a baby.

I have two favorite Boat stories: "The Elaborate Bath" and "The Bat."

Funny, who was two years older than Boat, was delighted when she joined the household. He was still a young enough cat to want to play, while Cuddles, my older cat, was far too dignified to play with him. Cuddles was miserable, because Funny tormented her trying to get her to play. Boat solved that problem by spending hours playing all sorts of cat games with Funny and then curling up with him to sleep.

One day, when Boat was perhaps a year old, I was reading in bed, with Boat for company. She was taking one of those elaborate cat baths, the kind where you wash carefully between your toes and spend ages washing behind your ears. Funny came to join us and watched as Boat took her bath. As she was carefully grooming the soft fur on her tummy, he stretched himself out beside her and moved his head and neck between her and the area she was washing. She looked at him a minute then obligingly washed his head and neck with the same degree of thoroughness she had been using on herself. He purred and turned his head this way and that to allow her to clean every inch of his head. His eyes were closed as she washed the underside of his neck.

Finished, she went back to grooming herself. Funny opened his eyes, sized up the situation, and slid over so that now his belly was under her mouth. Boat stopped grooming and considered what she wanted to do next. She then gave his belly a few perfunctory licks, stopped briefly, and then bit him quite firmly in the center of his belly. His eyes opened again, met hers, and he moved over on the bed to allow her to complete her twice interrupted bath. When she finished, they curled up together, with her head on his neck, and fell asleep.

The bat entered the house late one evening near the end of August 1997 by way of the deck off the bedroom that Mark and I use. The contractor built the deck when he repaired our roof, replacing the dilapidated deck that existed at that time. Mark had completely enclosed it with chicken wire, including over the top, so that Wicket could go in and out through a cat door. My cats have delighted in going out onto the deck. It is a good compromise, because I won't let them run loose for fear of them being injured.

During the day, the deck is a favorite sunning place, and at night, it becomes a place of adventure. On this particular night, I had thought that all the cats were out of the bedroom and was surprised when Boat came through the cat door at about eleven o'clock, making the little trilling noise that cats make when they are proudly presenting you with something they've caught. My glasses were too far away to reach, as was the light. I did reach the flashlight near the bed and could vaguely see that she was in the center of the room, with a small object by her foot. She touched it and it moved a couple of inches.

My imagination is somewhat limited … The only thing I could imagine a cat catching on a second-story deck completely enclosed with chicken wire at eleven was a bat. I do not like bats.

With dread lest it get away from her and fly around our small bedroom, I climbed out of bed and crept to the dresser and my glasses. To my great relief, I soon discovered that she had caught the first fall leaf. A huge, old, maple tree hung over our house, and leaves fell onto the deck in the autumn. My cats would carefully bring these leaves into the house and make piles of them in which to play, much like kids do on their front lawns. This was the first leaf to appear on the deck that fall, and Boat was evidently looking forward to the change of seasons more than I was. With a sigh of relief, I returned to bed, leaving her to play with her prize.

TRAVIS

Travis, another chestnut horse with white markings, and about five and a half feet high where the saddle rests, loved jumping. I loved jumping horses as a teenager but had absolutely no interest in jumping by the time Travis came into my life. For several years, I boarded him at a hunter/jumper stable, so it shouldn't be a surprise that my riding instructor gave me a jumping lesson.

What actually happened was that I was taking two lessons a week at that time: one for form (equitation) and one in a group to learn not to be so afraid to ride with other horses in the ring.

The other riders in the class were young women who were interested in learning how to jump. They often found our group equitation lesson boring. One day, they talked the instructor into including jumping in that evening's class. The instructor put up a very small jump, probably not even a foot high, out of cross poles (two poles that are higher on the outside end than the inside end, and cross to make a misshapen X). Before the jump, she laid two poles on the ground about a horse's length apart, so that the horses would have to trot over the poles to get to the jump. It was supposed to make the horse pay better attention to what was going on.

You need to have as background for this story that Travis very much enjoyed jumping and became quite animated when he knew that he was going to jump. You also need to know that the instructors at this stable made you spend about half of your equitation lesson trotting and posting with your feet out of the stirrups. That was no mean feat, because posting required you to raise your body out of the saddle in rhythm with the horse's gait.

Therefore, posting without your stirrups required you to hold your knees still against the horse and lift your body through the use of your inner thigh muscles alone. Initially, it was painful and exhausting, but it was considered an essential skill for jumping a horse. You were also taught not to look down and to keep your weight back in your saddle until the actual jump occurred, when you were to lean forward. And you were constantly told to keep your heels lower than your toes ("Heels down.")

Each of us that night took turns at trotting over the two poles and jumping the tiny jump, while the rest of the class had our horses stand quietly on the other side of the ring. By the third time I approached the jump configuration, Travis had figured out that we were jumping. His ears were pricked forward in happy anticipation, his body gathered under me, ready for my every cue.

As we trotted toward the jump, I made my first mistake. I looked down at the poles lying on the ground. That shifted my center of gravity forward, and like the well-trained horse that he was, Travis interpreted that as a command to go faster. To him, a signal to go faster when an obstacle was on the ground a few feet ahead meant that the obstacle was a jump. Travis took the two ground poles as a spread jump, which stretched his body as he jumped over them, and pulled me out of the saddle so that I was suspended over his shoulders. Now my toes were lower than my heels, so my stirrups slipped off my feet. They banged freely against Travis's sides. The extreme forward body position, plus the bumping, plus the horse's love of jumping, produced a horse that was now cantering (a faster gait than a trot) toward the jump, with his rider totally out of control and all the rein he wanted. Travis centered himself perfectly before the jump and soared over it as though it were show-jump height. On the other side of the jump, he continued to canter around the ring, so pleased with the whole process that he interspersed bucks between his canter strides for sheer exuberance.

Thanks to the balance and strength that I had developed by trotting and posting without my stirrups, I was able to bring the horse back under control despite the lack of bracing that the stirrups provide. So I learned from Travis, in about fifteen seconds, why you don't look down at a jump, why you keep your heels down, why you sit back in your saddle, and why you must learn to post without your stirrups if you are going to be a good hunter/jumper rider.

The instructor made me ride one more time over that jump course, just to prove to me that I had learned something that day. Travis was a good boy and did it perfectly that time, in no small measure due to my meticulous attention to the position of my body on the horse.

It was the last time I remember jumping. As far as I was concerned, that was my definitive jumping lesson, and the only one that I would ever require. If God had intended me to jump over fences, I would have been born a horse.

THE LAKE PLACID HORSE SHOW

You lose all credibility when you say that I sit a saddle elegantly. I have seen elegant, and neither Travis nor I qualify. At my best, I managed a little grace and perhaps style, but never elegance.

Travis might have been elegant with the right rider, but a more accurate description would have been powerfully graceful, in the same way that your favorite professional football broken-field runner could be described as such. From the point of view of the rider, he was like riding a powerful coiled spring. You could feel the power gathered under you and poised for action, his ears forward, alert to the world around him, yet somehow totally in touch with the rider so that the slightest change in position would produce action on his part.

Elegance was the professional rider and grand prix horse that I watched a number of years ago at the Lake Placid Horse Show. It's one of the top ten shows in the country for hunters and jumpers, and I went with a group of people one year to watch. I brought back three vivid memories, one of them my definition of elegance.

The rider was a tall, thin, blonde woman from this area, mounted on a tall, sleek, bay gelding with a white star on his forehead. She was surrounded by a circle of girls, perhaps eight to ten years old, who were worshipfully talking with her and petting her horse. The rider sat the horse in the bustle of the crowd at ringside with complete serenity, her reins slack. She sat with the same grace that a professional dancer has when she sits in a chair, looking simultaneously totally relaxed and totally perfect in posture, her head bent down to speak with the children. The horse, valued at more than my house, and gleaming in the sunlight, was also relaxed, with his head lowered to the level of the children so that they could stroke his face. They looked like my childhood mental picture of a royal couple giving an audience to their subjects. Both were gracious and charming, smiling—or the horse equivalent (perked ears)—at their admirers. Both were completely focused on the children.

The second memory is of a teenage boy from the stable where I boarded Travis, who was competing in a jumper class. The boy had recently transferred his horse from another stable to the one I used, because he was dissatisfied with his training and his horse. The boy's family wanted him to excel in the show ring and had paid a considerable price for the horse. But the more they competed in very minor shows, the worse they did. The horse was sour and often refused to jump, crashing through a jump or stopping or swerving at the last minute. They were seriously debating selling the horse.

The man trainer at the stable was working with the pair and had told the family that the boy and horse were a good match but were competing in the wrong types of shows. They were competing in the "hunter" classes, which are graded on perfection of form. The trainer believed that they belonged in the "jumper" class, where the grading is on speed and the height of the jumps.

The course is set by the judges, and you must take the jumps in a specific order, which sends you zigzagging around the ring. You are disqualified if you take the jumps out of order or omit one. Jumping competitions start and end by crossing a light beam, which activates a timer; the fastest time without knocking down jumps wins. If there is a tie, the tie is broken by a jump off, which involves repeating the course with the jumps raised until one of the horses knocks down a jump.

The trainer was so convinced that he was right that he entered the pair in a class at the Lake Placid show, the equivalent of taking someone off a schoolyard jungle gym and entering them in the Olympic trials. Both the boy and the horse were very nervous at ringside, watching people like the Firestones compete on fabulously expensive horses.

When it came their turn and the boy signaled to the horse to go, the lanky bay shot forward like a racehorse from the starting gate. About halfway through the course, the boy realized that he had almost left out a jump and turned the galloping horse toward it much too late. When the horse reached that fence, he was not perpendicular to it and, in fact, was nearly parallel to the crucial jump. Instead of refusing, the horse threw himself over the fence, scrambled to keep from falling as he spun around to get to the next fence, and completed the course without any faults and with a credible time (although not good enough to earn him a ribbon.)

When they had crossed the finish line and slid to an abrupt stop, the boy flung his arms around the horse's neck and hugged him. They had found their place in the show world and become a real team. As they walked away from ringside, the boy's father had his arm around his son's shoulders, the boy was petting his horse as they walked, and both father and son wore smiles of pride and delight.

The third memory is of watching the Firestone family for two days. Mr. and Mrs. Firestone competed in many classes, on a whole string of horses. (They had brought forty horses for them, their granddaughter, and a professional rider.) I was struck by how much fun they were having. It wasn't deadly serious to them, as it was to so many competitors. Yes, they were pleased when they did well, but it was obvious that winning was not first on their list of priorities. They enjoyed the riding for itself.

BEN

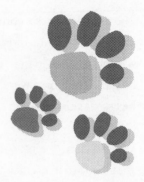

My younger son, in one of his crisis periods, asked why God was doing/ allowing such awful things to happen to him. Let me begin with the statement that my God is a loving God. Also, I am convinced that we create most of our own evil without the help of outside powers, good or evil. But sometimes, bad things do happen to good people/animals, and I can only turn to the story of Ben for a metaphorical answer to the eternal question: why?

Ben was twelve years old when his owners brought him in because of the lump on his shoulder. He was a big, brown tiger cat who came for regular checkups and vaccinations but was seldom sick. His owner had noticed a very fast-growing lump attached to his left shoulder blade and immediately scheduled an appointment. Both my associate veterinarian and I believed that it was a dreaded vaccination-induced fibrosarcoma.

Fibrosarcomas are a nasty kind of cancer identified in the 1990s as being caused by the cat's immune system overreacting to a vaccine. When I retired in 2008, veterinarians believed that the problem was restricted to killed vaccines. That means a vaccination of dead organisms, as opposed to a modified live vaccine, where the organisms are less able than normal to cause disease but still alive. The adjuvant, an inert material included in the vaccine to make the body react more strongly and therefore give better immunity, was believed to be the problem.

In 2014, researchers are less certain why a vaccine triggers fibrosarcomas. These tumors grow very rapidly, extend fingerlike projections into nearby tissue, and are extremely hard to cure surgically, because the surgeon can't see where the edges truly are. The current official recommendations for handling a vaccine-induced fibrosarcoma are the following:

1. Send a biopsy sample to a pathologist.

2. Do a CAT scan (no pun intended) if the diagnosis is confirmed.

3. Have a board-certified veterinary surgeon remove the tumor.

4. Follow up with radiation therapy.

You are still likely to lose the cat within a year. Of course, sometimes you do get lucky and are able to remove it all at surgery and the cat is cured, but not often. Two or three cats in my practice survived fibrosarcoma cancers, but I lost more than I saved.

Ben's people and I discussed the options, and it was decided to have me remove the tumor to the best of my ability and let the pathologist confirm the diagnosis from what I had removed. This would be Ben's only chance at survival. CAT scans, surgical specialists, and radiation therapy were not options.

My associate veterinarian and I took out all the tissue we dared. In unpolished language, we made the biggest, deepest hole we thought we could close, leaving enough muscle, we hoped, to let Ben continue to use his leg. I'm pretty brave; I did two weeks of independent study in plastic and reconstructive surgery in the 1980s. It was a *big* hole, about the size of a lunch plate, and included a muscle layer below the tumor. We even took a little of the covering (periosteum) off the bone, although we didn't take any bone from the shoulder blade. The pathologist confirmed the diagnosis and told us that the margins were clean (no visible cancer cells), although the deep margins were closer to the cancer cells than you like to have them.

So the metaphor? Well, Ben hurt after this surgery, even with pain medication. And he was never able to understand why his family brought him to me, or why I hurt him. He healed without a limp, and we saved his life, but I bet he had some unhappy memories. And I suspect that there are oftentimes when we are Ben, and God is the surgeon, and there is no way to explain why.

FROSTY

Not many years before I retired, on a bitterly cold winter day, one of my clients brought in a cat that she had found lying on the ground next to her garage. She had seen the scruffy-looking cat hanging around for a day or so but couldn't take it in because her husband was (literally) deathly allergic to cats. Now she felt bad, because she thought the cat was dead.

One of my assistants took the box with the motionless cat from her and touched its eye to see if there was brain activity. The cat didn't respond. Then it took a shallow breath. Mike raced it back to me. Its faint heart beat much too slowly, it breathed only once or twice a minute, and its temperature was too low to register on the thermometer. We began a warm intravenous drip and wrapped it in warm towels. We placed the comatose cat in a kennel under a heat lamp and waited.

The cat actually revived and began to eat a few hours later.

Unfortunately, its emaciated body had several abscesses hiding under the matted fur. Legally, that made it a rabies exposure case. We cleaned up the wounds, began antibiotic treatment, and drew blood for FIV and feline leukemia testing. Happily, the cat tested negative for both viruses.

We named the cat Frosty and moved her into quarantine, where she lived for six months.

From her point of view, she had woken up in heaven. She was warm and had an unlimited amount of food, since quarantined cats are handled as seldom as possible and have a self-feeder and self-water system in their cages. We tried to make the cage comfortable and constructed it out of two very large dog crates, stacked one above the other. The upper area had a shelf and a hammock, while the lower area had a litter box and the food and water. This double cage was locked inside an indoor run, so that there was no way for an unauthorized person or an animal to contact the quarantined cat.

Frosty spent her six months happily eating and sleeping. She grew positively fat, and her long hair grew back to cover all the places we had shaved because of mats or wounds. Not only was she sweet tempered, she was a beautiful cat.

Over the next six months, we treated her abscesses and dewormed and vaccinated her. When she had completed her time in quarantine, we spayed her and gave her to Alice, who renamed her Heidi, because she looked like a Norwegian Forest cat. Her life as an abandoned cat ended, and her life as a pampered, much loved indoor cat began.

JONEE

All the clinic mascot dogs had died by the time Mrs. Ryan brought Jonee and her siblings to the office for their first exam and vaccinations. Her grandmother had been my Folly's granddaughter. Our office manager urged me to buy the puppy to be the clinic mascot, and I was gullible enough to make the purchase.

Jonee was a black Lab, sweet, and playful. But I wasn't really ready then to love another dog and turned the care and training of the puppy over to my staff. They taught her to be housebroken, to not venture into the lab/pharmacy or waiting rooms without permission, and to lie under the receptionist's counter to sleep. She had the run of the business office, which included our kitchen area, and ate lunches with the staff. She played in the side yard and swam in the pond. When people came into the waiting room from the parking lot, she greeted them by putting her front feet on the counter so they could reach over and pet her. (This was something all the clinic mascot dogs and the dogs of my staff learned to do, because sometimes the "visitors" would give them dog cookies, and most "visitors" would pet them.) It was a pretty good life for a dog.

But my staff worried that the puppy would be lonely at nights and on the weekends and that she wouldn't housebreak as fast if she was crated too much, so Kim and Kelly took turns taking her home. Over time, she ended up going primarily with Kelly, where she slept on the bed and was generally spoiled by both Kelly and her husband, Kevin. She made enough trips to McDonald's and Burger King that she recognized those names and would get excited when the names were spoken. She knew that she would be given a hamburger of her own. From her point of view, Kelly was her person, and she belonged to Kelly heart and soul.

For a while after Jonee chose Kelly, I pretended that the dog was still mine. But when Kelly stopped working at the clinic full time, I admitted publicly that the dog was actually hers, and Jonee moved into Kelly's house for good. Kelly was her first and strongest love, but Kevin came in a close second. She was a true Labrador, totally devoted to her family.

Whenever Kelly was working at the clinic, Jonee would come with her. She always acted like there had been no gap in their coming, settling into the old routine of greeting clients, sleeping on the business office couch or under the receptionist's desk, and playing with the dogs the other employees brought to work. She never ventured out of the allowed areas.

As an old dog, Jonee developed diabetes and became blind. She took her insulin shots twice daily and was still very much herself, continuing to act as she always had at the clinic. She would be in the business office if Kelly was there, and tried to mooch lunches from the staff. She never went into the lab/pharmacy area without permission, stopping at the doorway, as she had been trained, to see if someone would invite her in. She slept under the receptionist's desk and greeted clients. She played in the side yard with the dogs that belonged to the staff. When Kelly and Kevin built their dream house, they had to watch her carefully when they were all outside, because she would take off down the long driveway to go visit the nearest neighbor.

Sadly, Kelly died of cancer less than a year after they had moved into the new house, and Jonee left us to be with Kelly a year or so later. They were an unforgettable pair, both of them cheerful, playful, and loving to the very end.

PROTECTIVE DOGS

In 2008, two of the most popular breeds were Rottweillers and Pit Bulls. They are part of the growing belief that to be safe in your home, you need a large, aggressive dog. I'll grant you that there are nice dogs in both breeds, but I have seen too many nasty ones to be enthusiastic when I encounter a new dog of either breed. After I know that your dog is nice and trustworthy, that's a different story. What people don't seem to understand is that a dog doesn't have to be nasty to be protective, especially in an unusual situation.

For the past forty-five years, I have owned Labrador Retrievers. My first Lab was named Jack. When we were cleaning out the abandoned building that became my veterinary clinic, a neighbor boy came over to help. He wanted to earn enough good will to be allowed to ride his snowmobile on the property that winter. Jack was an oversize Lab. He was the result of two neighbor dogs of the same breed having a litter, with no further thought to quality than that.

I was given Jack as a present, and he was a wonderful dog, even if he was too big. What was more to the point, he outweighed the neighbor child, and his head was at the level of the boy's chest. The boy was helping to shovel years of debris off the floor, and at one point placed the shovel over his shoulder and walked across the room toward me. Jack, who didn't know the boy, interpreted the behavior as threatening. He broke the chain that I was using to keep him away from the broken glass that was littering the floor and charged the boy, growling fiercely. The boy froze in terror.

Fortunately, Jack was not nasty by nature and was well trained in obedience. I shouted in my most authoritative voice, "Jack, no!"

The dog instantly stopped (about five feet from the boy) and turned and came to me, looking very sorry for his mistake. I reassured both him and the neighbor, and everything ended well because Jack was nice dog at heart.

Many years later, my teenage babysitter called her father late one evening to ask him to bring her something. Thinking he was expected, he walked in my kitchen door without knocking. At that point, I owned two Labs: a yellow female named Folly and her black son named Matty. These dogs slept on the beds with my sons, who had learned to walk by hanging onto them. Matty had been shown in obedience trials. He worked with either voice commands or hand signals but hated showing. His idea of fun was to spend the day with me. Folly had been a conformation, or "breed' show dog who loved showing and was a real ham. She liked to pretend she was a "dumb blonde" whose only job was to look beautiful and would merely cock her head and look at you if you told her to "sit", "down", or "stay". But she had taught herself hand signals by watching Matty work and would do "sit", "down", and "stay" in response to hand signals.

Both Folly and Matty were happy-go-lucky dogs, and the babysitter had never seen them do anything but wag their tails and lick people. In this instance, however, they didn't know the large man who had just walked in unannounced, with only a teenage babysitter and two small children home. My goofy Labs pinned the father to the wall next to the back door, hackles up, teeth bared, until the babysitter arrived and told them "no!" Once they knew that he was welcome, they were just as friendly as normal.

The sitter told me when I returned that she had not expected them to be protective and that she would never be afraid to be alone in my house. If the intruder had been a stranger, he would not have moved until she had called the police and they had arrived to take over from the dogs.

A TIME TO REPORT? IF YES, TO WHOM?

Our society is more aware of the need to protect animals (and people) from abuse than it was years ago. I firmly believe that is a good thing. But care must be taken not to criminalize all acts of neglect, since it is possible for life to get out of our control. When I was a child, the expression was "When you act, you should follow the rules, and when you judge, you should allow for the exceptions."

Today, allowing a collar to remain on a growing puppy too long and become imbedded in the puppy's neck is an act punishable by law. But I have seen it happen to animals that are beloved and otherwise well cared for when a person buys a fast-growing, giant breed of dog, such as a Saint Bernard. That is especially true if the pup has long hair. Is the owner solely to blame, or are the veterinarian and breeder also liable? This is an issue of ignorance and should be dealt with through education, not criminalization.

How about ingrown toenails? It is not uncommon to have pets brought into veterinary offices because they are limping and the cause is an ingrown nail. If the cat is difficult to handle, and hard to transport, should the owner be taken to court if a nail becomes ingrown? Or should the veterinarian be expected to find a way to help the owner get the nails done on a regular basis, through sending a technician team to the house, recommending a groomer who will make house calls, or teaching the owner ways to safely transport the pet to the hospital?

What about the elderly owner whose pet is totally flea infested? The house will be infested too. We once sent a technician to one person's home to help with flea control and discovered that the person needed help in other areas of life. Adult protective services was called and helped the owner.

If you are kind in your approach, owners who are not properly caring for their pets will usually be receptive to education regarding proper care, or actual help in caring for their pets, or even help in finding the pet a new home. It is a known fact that in households where women are being abused, their pets are often being abused as well. Those women do not need to be criminalized but need help in escaping from a desperate situation. I am proud to have been told by two such women that I was instrumental in helping them and their pets begin new, safe, lives.

Many years ago, I had a dog breeder in the practice who was producing exceptionally nice puppies. Then her life fell apart. Her husband filed for divorce. Her child became deathly ill. She had horses, dogs, and cats to care for, but her energy was all going into caring for her child. Was that wrong?

It became obvious to us that her animals were being neglected in significant ways. Instead of calling the police and reporting her for abuse/neglect, my associate veterinarian took it upon himself to volunteer to go to her home twice daily to care for her animals. She was understandably grateful and turned the care of her pets over to him until she was able to care for them herself, which was a significant period of time.

At his suggestion, she permitted us to find new homes for the majority of her animals. She didn't need to be taken to court; what she needed was compassionate, practical help. Eventually, her child recovered, and she resumed the responsibility of caring for her animals. Later, she remarried and moved away.

A number of years after that, one of my clients came in to the clinic with a new puppy. It was one of the happiest, healthiest puppies I have ever seen, and a beautiful example of its breed. The owner told me that the breeder said hi. She had purchased the puppy from the woman who had needed our help when her child was sick.

WACKY

People often ask me, "How long do cats live?" It's a good question. The record in our clinic for documented age was twenty-five years, and the cat's name was Wacky.

Wacky was a gray cat that belonged to a client named Mr. Knight and first came to my practice as a little kitten. One of the things that happens when you are in practice in a small community for many years is that you see the circle of life. Pets and owners grow old and die; babies are born and new puppies and kittens come into homes. One reason that I stayed a "family doctor" and didn't become a specialist was because there is comfort in being part of that circle. It always made me sad when people never got another pet after one died. There is much comfort in new life when you don't expect it to "replace" what you have lost, but instead to be a totally new blessing.

So the years passed for Mr. Knight and Wacky and Angel, a white cat about five years younger than Wacky. Wacky was thirteen when Mr. Knight was no longer able to stay in his own home and asked me to try to place the two cats. Everyone who deals with cats knows how hard it is to place anything but a kitten. Kittens are adorable. If you are a cat person, adult cats are beautiful and charming. But cat people often are already at their "catpacity" from taking in homeless kittens. I was delighted and relieved when Greg and Phyllis Silver asked me if I knew of any older cats that needed homes. They took Wacky and Angel, and everybody was happy for about six years.

Then the Silvers were faced with entering assisted living and asked me to place all three of their pets. Princess, the dog, went to Pat, who had taken Omar. I kept Wacky and Angel as clinic mascots. After all, Wacky was nineteen then, and I thought, *How long can a cat live?* For six years, Wacky and Angel lived at the clinic and hung out in the business office during the day. He had medical issues that required daily medication, but that was no problem as far as we were concerned. At twenty-five, his body just wore out, and we reluctantly put him to sleep. Angel lived almost a year after Wacky died, and we lost her to cancer at twenty.

So how long *do* cats live? Most feral cats live about three years. Outdoor cats with homes generally go about six years. Indoor-outdoor cats live a little longer. Strictly indoor cats usually live fifteen to twenty years. Yes, there are exceptions to the rule, but most cats live a lot longer if you keep them inside. If you love them, keep them in.

AT MIKE'S REQUEST

When Rusty came in, Mike Rice had been working for me for a couple of years. Mike dreamed of going to veterinary school. Rusty was a stray, nondescript, brown tiger cat that was hanging around a client's home. The client's other cats weren't especially happy about the situation, but the Harris family just couldn't let Rusty starve. After several days of coming for meals, Rusty disappeared. When he reappeared almost a week later, he looked really sick. Mr. Harris brought him to me for examination.

When I first saw Rusty, he was emaciated, dehydrated, and having some difficulty breathing. His abdomen was so empty that his belly wall was almost touching his backbone. Radiographs confirmed my suspicions; Rusty had been hit by a car and had a diaphragmatic hernia. In plain English, when he was hit by the car, the force of the blow had torn the diaphragm (the muscle wall between the chest and the abdomen) and the abdominal organs were now in the chest.

Diaphragmatic hernia repairs are difficult, high-risk surgeries. You take an animal that is already having trouble breathing and anesthetize it. Most of the lungs already are unable to inflate because the abdominal organs are in the way. Now the cat can't position itself to keep the little lung that is functioning on top of the heavy abdominal organs.

As soon as the anesthesia takes effect, you have to forcefully push air into the lungs, because the cat can't inflate the lungs itself. But breathing for the cat is an art. If you push too hard, you will overinflate the lungs and damage them. If you don't push hard enough, there won't be enough oxygen exchange to keep the cat alive. On top of this, the cat is already dehydrated and its system stressed with low oxygen levels, electrolyte imbalances, and whatever injuries have occurred to the displaced organs.

As soon as you open the abdomen, you have also effectively opened the chest. Usually, two people have to be scrubbed into the surgery (a surgeon and a surgical assistant, who holds things out of the way while the surgeon works). You need a third person to breathe for the animal, and perhaps a fourth to get the surgeon supplies (such as suture material) and add medications to the IV drip that runs throughout the surgery.

I explained to Mr. Harris what was involved, that I preferred to refer such cases to the surgical specialist, and that there would be considerable expense involved. He couldn't see investing what could easily be a thousand dollars in a stray cat, and we discussed euthanasia as the kindest alternative. Neither of us thought letting the cat die of suffocation was an option.

At this point, Mike spoke up. It would be a shame to euthanize the cat when we could perform a surgery that would cure him. Besides, Mike wanted to see the surgical repair done, since it is an uncommon surgery and you never know what you'll have to do until you are looking at the organs and can see what damage has occurred. Mike was willing to donate his time to be surgical assistant. He was sure that Kim would be willing to donate her time as technician, and that he would be able to talk Mark (my husband) into being the one to get from the shelf anything that Kim hadn't prepared in advance. If I would donate my time and the materials, we could save the cat. When Kim confirmed that she would stay after hours for free to breathe for, monitor, and medicate the cat, I knew that I was hooked.

Mark and Jane, a friend and client who happened to be in the office that evening, acted as gofers and an audience, while Mike, Kim, and I did the surgical repair. The surgery lasted a couple of hours, with Kim breathing for the cat most of that time, by squeezing a bag on the gas anesthesia machine.

She monitored his heart and lungs with a stethoscope that is designed to slide down the cat's esophagus to the level of the heart.

The cat's liver, stomach, spleen, and small intestine were all in the chest. There were many places where those organs were adhered (stuck with newly forming scar tissue) to injured areas in the chest and on the torn diaphragm. Working from the abdominal side of the diaphragm, Mike and I very gently freed all the abdominal organs from their adhesions and returned them to normal positions in the abdomen. We closed the tear in the diaphragm and then the abdominal incision.

As we were closing, we put in place a chest drain tube, with a Heimlich one-way valve tube attached so that air and fluid that might leak from the damaged lungs could drain out and not collect in the chest to compromise lung function.

We stayed to monitor the cat until he was fully awake and breathing well on his own, which was about nine o'clock, then went to dinner at a local restaurant, leaving Mike to monitor the cat.

At eleven o'clock, we returned, bringing Mike dinner. And then we checked the cat and went home for the night. Mike continued to monitor Rusty until three in the morning, and then he too went home to get some sleep.

When Rusty was alert and eating the day following surgery, with very little drainage from the chest tube, we were pretty confident that he would be okay.

After three days, we removed his chest drain. Rusty went home with Mr. Harris but wasn't accepted by Mr. Harris's cats and was ultimately placed with another client. He is now living in the lap of luxury, with an owner who adores him.

Mike went on to veterinary school, where he was given an award for his surgical skills. After graduation, he worked in a veterinary emergency hospital, then returned to the area and bought a veterinary hospital.

Kim worked for me until I retired and now works for "Dr. Mike." She was and is an exceptionally good technician. Kim and I never lost an animal during surgery, including several diaphragmatic hernia repairs, in the seventeen years that we worked together.

Everyone involved—the Harris family who took pity on the cat initially, Jane and Mark who got to see an amazing surgery, me, and especially Rusty— were thankful that I employed people like Mike and Kim. Their compassion was exceeded only by their skills and enthusiasm.

NEW DISCOVERIES

It is 2014 and I've owned the lake house for twenty-nine years, but we are still discovering new delights of nature. About nine years ago, we saw our first hummingbird moth. It behaves like a hummingbird, hovering around the red bee balm flowers like a little helicopter as it drinks nectar from the blossoms. It is small and brown, but if you are lucky enough to get a good picture of one, you discover that it has transparent "windows" in its wings. I looked up the little moth and discovered that the caterpillars feed on verbena. That is a shrub with white flowers that grows wild in our area. As a matter of fact, I have a lovely one at the edge of the road. The white flowers are arranged in a circle on the branches and make beautiful cut flowers early in the spring.

In the fall of 2007, we made another discovery. It had been an especially warm fall, with no frost through October. One rainy night, as he was walking the dogs before bedtime, my son Joe discovered a large salamander in the middle of the road. We had never seen one like this before. He was almost as long as a man's hand, with a black body and bright orange spots along his sides. Because this is the age of computers, Joe went online and searched for salamanders. He found a couple of excellent websites and we learned that we had a spotted salamander. Evidently, they are rarely seen because they come out only at night and live in burrows during the day. They lay their eggs in water but spend the rest of their lives on land. After taking his picture, we released him at the edge of the woodlot.

I was especially pleased to know that there are salamanders that I don't see here at the lake, because there are fewer of the ones that I do see. We have the orange newts that I occasionally find under rocks or logs as I garden. Twice a year, there is a mass slaughter of them as they cross the road. It always breaks my heart, and I move any live ones that I see crossing the road, hoping that they really did want to go in the direction in which they were headed. There are also greenish-brown ones that flock along the shoreline in the spring mating season and can be seen occasionally in the water during the summer and early fall.

Another new discovery for me was the fisher. I saw my first one cross the road near the lake in the spring of 2007. They are beautiful weasels, larger than ferrets, and jet black. My woodsman friend tells me they were common in the Adirondacks when he was growing up there, and are quite ferocious. Seeing one so near the house makes me glad that I keep my cats indoors, as fishers are known to eat cats.

As the population of our country spreads out to make suburbs of formerly rural areas, more and more kinds of wildlife are showing up on our doorsteps. Some are there because we moved into their home territories, and some move into ours as other wildlife are crowded out of formerly wild areas. We are being given the opportunity to discover animals and birds in our yards that are new to us, and to learn to live in harmony with them. I have learned not to have birdfeeders or leave pet food outside, or to let my dog run loose because there are opossums, raccoons, coyotes, and bears nearby. In turn, the wild predators and scavengers have learned to avoid my yard because I have dogs and no readily available food. It is a peaceful, respectful relationship that works for both them and me.

TIGER

Tiger was a small, black cat with an attitude. She was first brought to me as a geriatric cat in need of a second opinion.

One of the major improvements in veterinary medicine over my career has been in the area of pain control. In 2014, we have good pain medications for pets and can provide significant pain control for short-term situations like surgery or injuries as well as long-term situations like arthritis. Tiger had a major arthritis problem, but this was not 2014 and we didn't have a lot to offer. Her primary care doctor had recommended euthanasia as the only way to deal with her pain. Mrs. French didn't want to give up Tiger, despite her being very difficult to deal with in veterinary hospitals, and brought her to me for a second opinion.

Second opinions are a valid part of medicine, both human and veterinary, and a good doctor isn't offended when a patient seeks a second opinion for a serious problem. If the second doctor confirms what the first has said, it can strengthen the doctor-patient relationship. If a second doctor is able to more clearly communicate, or has knowledge that the first doctor lacks, the patient benefits. Today, when specialists are readily available, it is usually better to seek a second opinion from a specialist.

Because Tiger had nothing to lose, I recommended that we try giving her a daily dose of cortisone, if Mrs. French could get it in the cat without being hurt. She felt that she could, and we sent her home with some tablets. She was successful in getting the pills in the cat (I believe she crushed them into Tiger's food) and the medication made a huge difference in Tiger's pain level and her ability to get around the house. We adjusted the dose, and even changed the type of cortisone at one point. The cat was fortunate in that she never developed any of the possible life-threatening side effects to the drugs we administered. For many years, she came to the hospital for her annual visit and took cortisone on a daily basis.

Mrs. French was as nice as the cat was difficult, and because of respiratory problems, she was not supposed to have a pet at all. She had agreed with her doctor that Tiger would be her last cat, so the extra years gained by pain control had been a real blessing to both her and Tiger.

We were all pleased that Tiger had been able to live comfortably well into her teens, dying not long before I retired. Mrs. French brought me a black cat plant hanger and a beautiful donkey's tail plant to hang from it. They hang on my sun porch, and, as she requested in the card that accompanied the gift, when I see it I "think of Tiger, even though it doesn't hiss, spit, or curse."

THE FAWN

For many years, I worked to establish a garden area behind the clinic building. The property had been a gravel pit and then a drive-in theater. There was no topsoil, so I created the garden by patiently piling the manure from my horse stall in rows. As it decomposed, it became the area where I planted my crops. Because it was such a low area, it usually stayed damp in the summer, providing me with luscious tomatoes, hefty pumpkins, greens, corn, and squashes of several kinds. Recently, I added apple trees and raspberry bushes. Like Topsy, "it just grew" and became defined by three hundred or more feet of deer fencing.

Because the garden was so large, and because I preferred to mulch rather than put down black plastic, the weeds always got ahead of me. In an early evening during the summer of 2007, I was trying to find the squash and onions under all the weeds, when I heard a bleating sound like sheep make. I could hear the animal approaching the fence through the waist-high weeds and soon could see the weeds moving. To my amazement and delight, a wobbly, spotted fawn that couldn't have been more than a day old emerged by the fence right where I was working. It tried to come to me through the fencing and cried pitifully as it moved back and forth along the barrier.

I knew enough not to touch it, although the urge to "rescue" it was very strong. For perhaps five minutes, I remained where I was, weeding and watching, not even ten feet from the fawn, before I heard the second animal. This new noise was a very loud huffing noise unlike anything that I had ever heard. We had foxes near the garden and sometimes raccoons, but this wasn't either of them. I prayed that it wasn't a predator, because I wouldn't have been able to go to the gate and back down the outside of the fence fast enough to rescue the fawn.

As I finished my prayer, the mother deer, ears pricked forward, nostrils flared, appeared at the edge of the woods, only her head and neck visible above the weeds. She continued to call to her baby (or perhaps to warn me away) as she approached, and the baby continued to forlornly call to her. The doe's eyes never left me as she came right up to her fawn. I couldn't have been ten feet from them when she reached the fence and the fawn, turned, and together they silently slipped away through the weeds.

It was a magical experience.

BOB'S GIFT

This is not really a story about a cat as much as it is a story about people.

Bob came to my clinic a couple of years before I retired. His owner had just recently died, and the couple who brought him to me had taken him in to give him a little comfort before he was put to sleep. They had been friends with his owner and knew that she had spent a lot of time with him. When she went into the hospital at the end of her life, he was left home alone. Yes, he was fed daily, but he wasn't given much in the way of personal attention, since his owner was the focus of concern for all involved.

But now she was gone, and it just didn't seem right to Carol and John to have the old cat put to sleep without someone comforting him. He had obviously been distressed at his owner's disappearance, and their hearts went out to him. They had no pets of their own, so taking Bob home to live with them had seemed most appropriate. They brought him in to see me because he seemed uncomfortable due to constipation.

I suggested that we not only treat the constipation but also check kidney function, because constipation in old cats is frequently caused by dehydration from kidney disease. They agreed, and the tests confirmed my suspicion that Bob was a very sick geriatric cat in chronic renal failure.

We started Bob on treatment for his renal disease, consisting of fluid therapy, phosphate binders, and a diet that was a compromise between what the cat *should* eat and what he *would* eat. Bob would sit still while Kim or I placed the large needle under the skin of his back and ran in the five ounces of sterile fluids. He somehow knew when the right amount had been given and would start to walk across the exam table to John, so you had to be alert and stop the drip exactly at five ounces. While Bob had no real problem with Kim or me giving him the subcutaneous fluids, he was adamant that John and Carol not give them. That meant that they had to bring him to the hospital daily, even on weekends, for fluids. He did, however, allow them to administer his daily oral medication. Initially they had expected to treat him for only a few days, but the cat perked up with the fluids and had such a winning personality that they were reluctant to part with him. He was quite vocal, being Siamese, and clearly communicated, by actions and "words," his desires and needs. He enjoyed walking around their yard and took over their home as well as their hearts.

As usual, I attended the annual feline conference at Cornell Veterinary School that summer, and one of the speakers talked about high blood pressure in cats that were in renal failure. Taking blood pressures in pets was new. The equipment had only recently been adapted for cats and dogs, and few hospitals owned blood pressure measuring equipment. The speaker talked about the effects of high blood pressure in pets, including saying that they had headaches and blinked their eyes in a pain response. Bob had a peculiar habit that could be interpreted that way, instead of my interpretation, which was that he was having little "seizure-type activities" due to his high metabolic toxin level.

When I returned from Cornell with my brand-new blood pressure monitor, we checked his blood pressure, and sure enough, it was very high. We started him on blood pressure medicine, and he became much more active and visibly far more comfortable.

This loving couple faithfully brought Bob for daily fluids for nine months before we finally lost the cat to his kidney problem. They gave Bob nine months of love; Bob gave them a whole new loving family, because in that time the entire clinic staff came to consider Carol and John extended family. As the Bible says, "Love never fails." *New King James*—1 Corinthians 13:8

Although Bob is gone physically, the never-failing love that he brought into Carol and John's home remains in the deep friendship that Carol and I enjoy. Our friendship has not only survived but also grown, despite the loss of both Bob and John. And my retirement.

Likewise, in one sense, my practice ceased to exist when I retired, but in another sense, it remains like a daffodil that blooms then appears to be gone, only to reappear the next spring. The special people who mentored me in my lifetime became forever a part of who I am, how I live, and how I practiced veterinary medicine. Likewise, my heart, and the heart of my practice, still survives in the young people whom I mentored. Some were, or now are, veterinarians, and some went on to do other things.

The last two to become veterinarians are Dr. Michael Rice, who graduated from veterinary school in 2009, and Dr. Christina Marino, who graduated from veterinary school in 2012. They share my love of the medicine and the animals and the excitement of knowing that each day will be different; they will never lack for something new to learn. Mike also shares my love of surgery and is gifted in that aspect of veterinary medicine. Neither will be afraid to become connected to the people, nor to the beloved pets entrusted to their care.

Mike now owns a practice near where I live and is the doctor of my pets. Christina is remaining in academia and will become a specialist in internal medicine. They will take veterinary medicine forward into the future. Their knowledge and skills will far surpass mine. But our hearts are the same, and they are my legacy to the profession I loved.

In time, they will have their own *Mouse Tales* to tell.

As a wedding present, Mark and I received an original poem by Laura Saleem-Brodsky, who had written it especially for us. It ends with the following truth, which applies to life and work and friendships as well as marriages:

> Take heart for real love is like honey
> Which some beekeeper once told me stays forever